The Wealthy Barber

Everyone's Common-Sense Guide
to Becoming Financially Independent

David Chilton

Prima Publishing
P.O. Box 1260BK
Rocklin, California 95677
(916) 786-0426

Typography by Bookends Typesetting
Production by Janelle Rohr, Bookman Productions
Jacket Design by The Dunlavey Studio

Prima Publishing
Rocklin, CA

Library of Congress Cataloging-in-Publication Data

Chilton, David.
    The wealthy barber : Everyone's common-sense guide to becoming financially independent / by David Chilton.
      p.   cm.
    ISBN 1-55958-096-8
    1. Finance, personal.   I. Title.
HG179.C54 1991
332.024—dc.20   91-7659
                                              CIP

93 94 RRD 10 9 8 7 6 5 4 3
Printed in the United States of America

For information on ordering, see the forms in the back of this book.

To my family

About the Author

DAVID CHILTON is the president of a consulting firm that specializes in teaching financial planning techniques through employer-sponsored seminars. By combining common sense and humor, Dave has shown hundreds of thousands of people that sound financial planning is, indeed, "pretty simple stuff." A frequent guest on national TV and radio shows, and a much sought-after speaker, Dave lives in Kitchener, Ontario, with his wife, Susan, son, Scott, daughter, Courtney, and their wonder-dog, Charley.

Contents

Preface

THE WISEST TIPS ON HOW to develop a financial plan are of little use if they are not conveyed in an understandable manner—a manner that responds effectively to the questions and concerns of the reader. Likewise, the most articulately expressed thoughts on finance may be wasted if they are not presented in an entertaining style—a style that maintains the interest of the reader.

So how does one write an understandable and entertaining financial planning book?

I hope and believe that *The Wealthy Barber* answers that question by taking a "novel" approach to the teaching of financial planning.

Rather than inundating you with intimidating charts and graphs and a series of lifeless numbers, *The Wealthy Barber* will both entertain and inform you. Through fictional conversations between Roy Miller, our financial hero, and his barber shop patrons, you will learn that sound financial planning is not only relatively simple, but it can also be fun.

I wish you good reading and good planning.

David Chilton

Chapter 1

The Financial Illiterate

I LOVE APRIL. I WOULDN'T trade it for two of any other month. Except perhaps for October. Two Octobers would mean twice as many birthday presents—and Oktoberfests!

Why April? Weather-wise, it offers neither the best of summer nor the best of winter. It certainly doesn't provide the beauty of the fall months. Is it because, at least to poets and romantics, it symbolizes a new beginning, a kind of rebirth?

No.

I love April for three reasons: the National Basketball Association playoffs, the National Hockey League playoffs, and the essence of life itself—a new Major League Baseball season. Ah, April. Paradise on earth!

Thanks to my remote control, I can sit motionless, flicking back and forth between the Pistons on NBC and the Red Wings on channel 50, while listening to my beloved Tigers on WJR. When you throw in a second TV and a VCR, the possibilities are endless.

In addition to being professional sports' finest hour, April also ushers in the start of the golf season and marks the return of Michigan's fastest-growing religion: slo-pitch.

Needless to say, my wife, Susan, is not quite as fond of April as I am. However, even she would rank it among her favorite months. She is a fine tennis player, and April brings with it the first opportunity in half a year to hit the ball around. She also loves lawn work and spends a great deal of time in our garden. I use the word "our" loosely.

Surprisingly, slo-pitch season is something Susan enjoys as much as I do, if not more. The thirteen guys on our team range in age from twenty-eight to thirty-two, with me being the youngest. Seven are married and three have children. Tournaments, barbecues, pool parties, and evenings at our sponsor's—Banfield's Bar and Grill, a terrific bar in Ann Arbor—are the highlights of the summer. All the wives and girlfriends get along famously. In fact, they appear to hold contests to see who can sit in the stands and pay the least attention to the game. Inevitably, when a game ends, the first thing our devoted fans ask is "Who won?"

This April, though, is a little different from Aprils gone by. Sue is pregnant, or as she likes to put it, "we" are pregnant. If it's true that we are pregnant, it is also true that I am handling it better than Sue. I am seldom tired and I haven't gained a single pound over the first five months.

Actually, Sue is handling the pregnancy very well. She is a beautiful woman who prides herself on her appearance, so she has kept herself in excellent shape. As for being tired, no way. She's too excited. I'm sure every woman feels that way when she's about to have a baby, especially her first, but Sue is in a different league. One week after our doctor's confirmation, we had already bought a complete encyclopedia set. You never know when a child may feel a need to refer to an authority greater than his parent.

Our decision to have children was easy. Both Sue and I love kids. In a way, that's ironic because we both come from small families. Sue is an only child, and I have just one sibling. At thirty, my sister, Cathy, is two years older than I am, but because of our months of birth, she registered in school only one year before me. Much to everyone's surprise, I accelerated through the third and fourth grades and caught up to her. This is something I have never let her forget.

As I said, deciding to have children was easy. Barring unforeseen events, we plan on having three. Mind you, if they're all girls, we will keep on going indefinitely. When friends ask me what sex I hope this one is, I always reply, "I don't care . . . as long as it's a healthy boy."

Maybe I long for a son because I think that I could relate better to a boy and thus be a better parent. Maybe it's the old carry-on-the-family-name/I-want-to-be-immortal mentality. Then again, maybe Sue's right. It could just be so that I can play in the annual father-and-son golf tournament and miss another weekend of yard work each year. So much for Freud.

Without a doubt, the highlight of the pregnancy to this point has been the reaction of the four first-time grandparents-to-be. Each excited couple phones at least once every forty-eight hours to see how Susan feels and to make sure I'm doing the housework and treating her well. This wouldn't bother me if it were only her parents questioning my abilities as a husband, but my parents are even worse. Dad says that Mom fainted when Susan told her I shampooed the rugs, and I'm not at all sure he's kidding.

Truthfully, helping with housework has been a great learning experience—not a great experience, but a great learning experience. I now know the origin of the expression "A woman's work is never done." My wife, for example, works as a travel agent from nine till five, comes home, cooks a meal, does laundry, and works out. I can understand why she always hits the sack at ten-thirty. I've been out like a light by nine since I reluctantly volunteered to do some of the household tasks.

I can't defend my previous lack of respect for housework. And I don't have to. It's my mother's fault. The wife of a high school principal, she has never held a paying job.

As with most of their contemporaries, Dad brought home the bacon and Mom cooked it. While he was at work, Mom would do all the household chores, leaving her evenings free.

To my great pleasure, I was asked to do very little. While other kids mowed the lawn or shoveled snow, I chased down fly balls or played road hockey. I'm not sure why my parents were so easy on me, but to this day, I appreciate it.

On the other hand, Sue's parents, bucking the spoil-the-only-child stereotype, raised Sue to be a diligent worker. And to this day, I appreciate *that* even more! By the time we were married, she was used to doing housework and preparing meals. Being used to something, though, and enjoying it are far from synonymous. Now that I have come to realize just how much drudgery is involved in running a home, I am determined to become a *new and improved* person.

The guys on the slo-pitch team have started a pool, betting on how long the new me will last. Our pitcher informs me that the longest guess is four months—that is, until Sue is no longer pregnant. The shortest prediction, three weeks, was submitted by my wife. Now that's confidence.

As if taking it from the guys on the team two nights a week isn't bad enough, this weekend I'm going to get it from the future grandparents—live. As is our custom on the third weekend of each month, Sue and I are heading to Port Huron.

However, there's no need to feel sorry for us. Really. We go willingly. Both of us were born and raised there. No, Port Huron is not a household name, and no, it does not conjure up images of *Lifestyles of the Rich and Famous*. But despite that, it is also not the featureless town non–Port Huronites might imagine it to be—not at all.

In fact, Port Huron offers an unbeatable combination: growing economic prosperity, friendly people, and the beauty of life on Lake Huron. Originally discovered in the early 1700s by the British, today Port Huron is being rediscovered by everybody including auto industry suppliers, fresh-water sailors, Canadian firms expanding south of the border, and quality-of-life devotees.

If I seem defensive about Port Huron, it's because I am. In terms of national recognition, it certainly is no match for our current home, Ann Arbor. But there is something special about a hometown, especially one on the water. Port Huron comes alive in the summer. It's one continuous party, and to kids and teenagers that's pretty appealing.

Actually, that's pretty appealing to adults, too—us included. That's why this summer Sue and I are spending five weeks at a rented vacation home just north of Port Huron, in Lexington.

I've been teaching for six years now, and every summer I have either taken a course or taught one. But this year, with the baby due in early September, we elected to keep the summer open and head for the cool water.

Sue is ecstatic. There's a seasonal slowdown in her part of the travel business, cruises, so, like me, she has July and August off every year. Her friends, however, do not. So those summers that I've been studying, working, and golfing, she has often been forced to spend time alone, burning, peeling, and reading. I'm making it sound worse than it has been. As an independent woman, she has pursued several hobbies and interests. Nevertheless, she is really looking forward to seeing her two best friends and mother every day for five weeks this summer.

Initially, Sue's enthusiasm far outweighed mine. I have a great many friends in Port Huron, but only one of them is a teacher. Sure, Scott might be good for eighteen every morning—but who would I tee off with in the afternoons?

The more I thought about it, though, the more I liked the idea. My best friend, Tom Garrett, is taking a vacation from his job at the auto plant for the last three weeks of our stay. Tom loves to golf, go to Detroit Tigers games, lie on the beach, and quaff a few cold ones. In my book, the guy is perfect.

When Sue and I go to Port Huron for the weekend, we follow a fairly set routine.

We arrive Friday night at around eight-thirty. We usually go straight to my parents' house and enjoy a leisurely dinner. Then at ten-thirty, we go out to join some of our friends.

Saturday, Sue disappears. She does not save this act exclusively for Port Huron. In the four years we've been married, I've seen her only a dozen times on a Saturday afternoon—always at weddings. I'm not exactly sure where she goes, but it must be somewhere magical because invariably when she returns her shoes appear to have changed color.

While she is AWOL—Absent with Our Loot—I spend the day with Tom. We meet my sister, Cathy, for breakfast at the Thomas Edison Inn at nine o'clock sharp. Depending on what we did Friday night after leaving my parents, this is sometimes not painless.

Tom and Cathy have a curious, combative relationship. They remind me of Maddie and David on *Moonlighting*. They're always teasing and fighting, but it's obvious there's something there. As they're uninvolved and attractive people, it's surprising that they haven't at least tried going out together. But who am I to say? I thought Sonny and Cher were perfect for each other.

After breakfast, Cathy returns to her office to catch up on paperwork. She is the consummate American success story. In twelfth grade, she had the highest average in our graduating class. Both Michigan and Ohio State offered her generous scholarships. She decided that Michigan was perfect. It was close to Port Huron, and had a prestigious school of medicine. My parents were calling her Dr. Richardson before we'd even left high school.

However, not only did Cathy not become a doctor, but she also didn't even go on to college.

Knowing that her scholarship would cover most of her expenses, she felt no sense of urgency to get a summer job. Therefore, in the summer of grade 12, while I slaved at the brass company, Sis opened her own business. Combining her artistic flair with her love of horticulture, she founded Richardson Landscaping. The corporate name was simple, but the concept was pure genius.

Cathy spent the first four weeks of the summer combing the nicer neighborhoods in Port Huron. When she spotted a property that she felt would look better if landscaped differently, she would do a series of sketches until she perfected the *look*. While basking in the sun at the beach, she would do a watercolor of the final sketch.

The young entrepreneur would then frame the painting herself—tastefully, of course. A sticker on the back simply read "This is how Richardson Landscaping sees your home." The framed picture was delivered, via courier, to the homeowner. The total cost to Cathy was approximately $50 a picture.

Over the course of four weeks, she completed seventeen of these impressive and unique *business cards*. At the end of the month, Cathy started following up with phone calls, and she booked an amazing fifteen appointments.

At this point, I was still far from impressed. Four weeks into the summer, Cathy's venture was $850 in debt and I was constantly lending her money. As far as I knew, her scholarship did not include recompense for her brother.

Within a few days, though, I was no longer worried. I was jealous!

Cathy's pitch during the appointments was, to use my students' favorite word, "awesome." For a flat fee of $1,000, she offered to gather bids from four local landscaping firms, hire the winner, oversee all activities, and ensure that the job came in on time and on budget. There was no charge for her design.

Cathy's contagious enthusiasm, sound business proposal, and beautiful designs netted her six of the fifteen potential clients. Twelve years ago, $6,000 was an unbelievable summer job income. Today, $6,000 is an unbelievable summer job income!

She spent the rest of July and August supervising the six projects. Every customer was thrilled with the end result. Because she stayed on top of the landscaping companies, jobs actually came in at prices substantially under the norm. In essence, her services paid for themselves.

Referrals started pouring in and she has never looked back. Last year, working only eight months, she made more money than my father and I combined.

At first, it was difficult to accept the fact that my sister, a college dropout before she even got there, was "a mover and a shaker." However, when I saw the type of Christmas and birthday gifts that success translated into, I became fiercely proud of her.

Despite her great achievement, Cathy is still a one-woman operation, preferring to handle all typing, billing, accounts payable, and other clerical duties herself—Saturdays.

That's all right with Tom and me, because she wouldn't accompany us for the next item on our Saturday-in-Port Huron agenda, anyway. We go to the barber. That visit is one of the high points of the weekend. I'm sure most people don't think of a trip to the barber as a high point, but then again most people don't get their hair cut at Miller's Barber Shop.

Roy Miller started giving us "buzz cuts" when we were five years old. We've outgrown that style, but remained true to Roy. In addition to being intelligent and witty, he has the one quality that most endears a man to Tom and to me—he's a die-hard Tiger fan!

Like most barbers, Roy has a few Saturday regulars who are there only to pass the time. Two of the three, Jimmy and Clyde, don't have any hair left to cut. Clyde in particular gets a real kick out of our monthly visits. He is a big baseball fan, too—if you can be and cheer for the Indians.

During the warm-weather months, the next item on Tom's and my itinerary is golfing. Both of us love the game, but despite being reasonably good athletes who have played golf for several years, neither of us excels at the sport. I have a fifteen handicap, while Tom's fluctuates between sixteen and twenty-two, depending on whether he's trying to impress someone or entering a tournament.

Saturday nights in Port Huron hold something different each month. Sometimes we assemble for a house party or a ballgame. But most frequently, ten or fifteen of us descend on Chicken in the Rough, a popular and unique local bar with great chicken and even better beer.

Sundays, Sue and I go to church and out to brunch with her parents, whom I enjoy immensely. The Washburns have done quite well for themselves, owning and operating an industrial cleaning company. Like so many others, the company fell upon tough times in the early eighties. Unlike so many others, owing in large part to my in-laws' work ethic and its debt-free balance sheet, it weathered the storm.

I wouldn't call them rich, but well-to-do wouldn't be pushing it. They have a new home on the lake, a boat, and two nice cars. I don't think they have much in the way of investment assets, but because they have no debt, good cash flow, and a saleable business, their financial worries seem to be nonexistent.

After Sunday brunch, Sue and I head back to Ann Arbor. On the way out of town, we stop at Heaven's Gate Nursing Home. I still can't believe they named it that. Our only living grandparent, my grandmother, has been "waiting at the gate" for five years now. The doctors claim she is in excellent mental health, but I fear otherwise. Last week she predicted the Lions were going to win next year's Super Bowl.

9

Finally, we arrive back in Ann Arbor and spend Sunday evening recovering from the hectic weekend.

However, this upcoming weekend, our once-a-month routine will be slightly altered. On Friday, instead of going out after dinner, Sue and I are staying at my parents' so I can talk to my father. When I phoned him yesterday, I simply said that I needed to talk to him. I did not go into any details.

What a mistake! Mom called back five minutes later in hysterics. "Are Susan and the baby all right?" she demanded. "Are you all right? Did Cathy tell you something she hasn't told us? Are—"

To prevent my mother's impending coronary, I interrupted her barrage of questions and told her what I wanted to talk to Dad about—our finances.

Did it help? No. My mother persisted.

"Do you need money?" she continued shrilly. "Are you in trouble? Does this have to do with the time you—"

"No, Mom! I just need some basic financial planning advice."

"What led to this after all these years?" she asked skeptically. "What are you hiding from me?"

The fact is that when it comes to finances, I have nothing to hide. My lack of financial knowledge had really hit me for the first time just the other day. I was reading a local business publication when I stumbled across a "Self-Analysis Financial Planning Test."

No sweat, I thought. I'm a teacher. I don't fail tests; I fail students. Confidently, I picked up my pencil and set about responding to questions such as these:

- Have you selected the proper amortization period for your mortage?
- Is your will up-to-date?
- Could your dependents live comfortably in the event of your death?
- If you plan to retire early, have you set up a suitable savings program?

10

- How do you plan to pay for your children's education?
- Well over 50 percent of Americans retire in financial hardship. What are you doing to guarantee you won't be one of them?
- Are your debts structured properly?

Not only could I not give a satisfactory answer to many of the questions, but also I didn't even understand some of them. I caught an ominous glimpse of Susan, our sons, and me living as bag people.

I dropped my pencil, a worried man. It's not that I want to be a multimillionaire, although like everyone else, I do. I'll settle for being comfortable—very comfortable. I'd like to own a nice home and a vacation property, help my children get an education, and retire in relative affluence at a reasonable age. And I want to accomplish all of this without substantially sacrificing my present standard of living.

I think these goals are shared by most Americans. Are they realistic? Can they be realized on an average salary? If so, how?

Within an hour of reading that article, I was committed to learning the basics of financial planning. I had no desire to learn the intricacies of the stock market, nor was it my goal to be able to recite mortgage tables from memory.

All I wanted to know was how best to get where I want to be from where I am now.

I figured Dad is no financial genius, but he must have learned a few things in his fifty-eight years. He seemed as good a place as any to start.

Chapter 2

A Surprising Referral

THAT APRIL WEEKEND TRIP TO Port Huron changed my life.

The smell of my father's cigar, the voices of the Tigers radio announcers, and talks about saving money rather than spending it do not rank high on Sue's list of favorite things. Throwing them all together proved to be too much for her. Claiming fatigue, she retired early that Friday night. My mother also excused herself—not to go to bed, however, but to tackle the monthly chore of paying the bills.

Dad and I sat down to talk about something that in our twenty-eight years together we had never discussed before. In these days of open conversations about everything including sexual habits, money remains a taboo subject, even among family members.

"I can't believe we've never talked about money before," I marveled.

"Even if we had, it would have been a short conversation," Dad replied. "Up until six years ago, I didn't know a thing about finances. Your mother and I lived from paycheck to paycheck, making our mortgage payments, staying out of debt, and sometimes saving for things we wanted. The only thing your grandparents really told me about money management was not to borrow.

"We couldn't teach you what we didn't know, and your grandparents couldn't teach us what they didn't know. I don't think it's our fault as a family. I suspect most people have the same problem, and I blame it partly on our education system.

"Six years ago, when I finally learned the basics of financial planning, I couldn't believe how straightforward they were. It's just common sense. If I had looked into the fundamentals thirty years ago, or even fifteen years ago, your mother and I would be very well off today."

"And I'd love you even more than I do now," I interjected. "But Dad, for someone who didn't know much, you seem to have done all right."

"All right," he echoed, "but not great. And the frustrating part is that I now know great is achievable . . . easily achievable. It's incomprehensible to me that our state has not altered the school curriculum to include a basic family-finance course. All high school graduates should know how to fill out an income-tax form properly. They should know how to select their mortgage, how to finance their children's education, and how to save and plan for retirement.

"You know me, David. I've always been a big believer in public education, but that doesn't mean it can't use improvement. There's no debating the fact that one of the most crucial improvements would be to teach basic money skills. Hell, we're raising generation after generation of financial illiterates. I don't think that even the politicians understand the tremendous benefits the economy would enjoy if Joe and Mary Average knew how to handle their money properly."

"Dad, why did you—"

"I can't believe Sparky is leaving Frank Tanana in the game," Dad interrupted. "They're pounding him!" he added, as he rose to put the dog out.

As Dad left the room, I realized just how right he was. Sparky should have taken Tanana out.

He was also right about most Americans being financial illiterates. There is no excuse for our possessing as little financial knowledge as we do. When even a college-educated person like me is embarrassed by an elementary financial test, something is wrong. Although I'd never thought about it before, Dad was also right about the fault lying with our education system. I teach history and geography, but I have to admit that being able to date the arrival of Columbus at 1492 is of little consequence compared to being able to create a proper savings program. Both forms of knowledge are important, and a balance must be found.

Dad re-entered the room to a Frank Tanana game-ending strikeout. "Boy, is he a clutch pitcher, a great competitor," he beamed. "Big win, big win."

"How did you even manage to do 'all right' without knowing anything?" I continued.

"I'm not sure I like the way you phrased that," Dad replied with a laugh. "I brought home a fairly good income and we didn't have an extravagant lifestyle. Heaven knows you never wanted for anything, but we had no investment assets at all. Often we didn't have any more than a couple of hundred dollars in the bank.

"Our only hard-and-fast rule was not to borrow. If we needed a new car, wanted to go on a trip, or had to put a new roof on the house, we would save the money first. If we didn't have anything specific on our 'wish list,' we spent our entire monthly income. That was our complete 'financial plan,' so to speak."

"You borrowed to buy the house, though?"

"Oh, yes, obviously, we had to borrow to buy the house. We assumed a thirty-year mortgage," Dad answered. "Actually, six years ago, a lot of things came together. We made our final mortgage payment. You were graduating, and except for not being able to make your own bed and cook, you were becoming self-sufficient. Our income increased significantly through my textbook sales, and your uncle died and left your mother twenty-two thousand dollars.''

"I didn't know that!" I exclaimed, surprised.

"We wanted to surprise you by leaving you more than just the house. You know, something to help you get over the inevitable trauma of losing the two greatest influences on your life.''

"Yeah, yeah," I said, rolling my eyes.

"Anyway, when all those things happened at once, it became painfully obvious that I needed some financial advice. We had more than a thousand dollars a month to play with and almost twenty-two thousand dollars sitting in the bank. I was ten years from retirement and both your mother and I figured we'd better seek professional help.

"I just didn't want to do something stupid. I knew that with my pension plan, my retirement looked pretty good. But I also knew that if I handled our new-found nest egg and our monthly surplus funds well, your mother and I could be looking at a vacation home, a boat, some trips, or maybe even all of these. Both of us had always wanted a place on the lake and this was our chance.''

"So, what did you do? Something intelligent, I hope, considering that someday all this could be mine.''

"What about your sister? Don't you think it's only fair to leave her half?''

"Jackie Onassis? C'mon, Dad, it's pocket change for her," I joked. "What did you do?''

"I got the best haircut of my life," he deadpanned.

"Get serious, Dad. I really—''

"I am serious. I was down at Roy's one Saturday and I started talking to James Murray. You know James . . . He's always there on Saturdays with Clyde and Jimmy.''

"I know him well.''

"Well, what you probably don't know is that before he became so successful selling real estate, he did stints as both a stockbroker and a life insurance agent. I told him I was in the market for some financial planning advice and asked him if he could recommend anyone. Even though he had been out of the field for about ten years, I figured he would still know someone competent.

"He smiled and said, 'The best financial planner in town is holding a razor to your throat.'"

"Roy? C'mon," I said, disbelieving.

"I'm not kidding and neither was James. Over the next several months, as he cut my hair, Roy taught me the basics of financial planning. And you'll be pleased to hear that right now my finances are in great shape, and they're looking better all the time."

"You're right. I am pleased to hear that. But how the heck does a barber become a financial planning expert?"

"The answer to that, and in fact Roy's background in general, is quite interesting. As you know, Roy and I were high school classmates. He was the all-American boy. You know what I mean . . . good-looking, athletic, bright, funny. Everybody liked Roy. He was our class valedictorian and was voted most likely to succeed.

"He had always talked about being a lawyer, so naturally he was U of M–bound as a first step—"

"There are other universities, Dad," I interrupted.

"Only in your mind, son. Anyway, Roy and I lived in the same residence at college, but I didn't see him much. Between studying, playing varsity basketball, and coming home to visit his girl friend, he was a busy guy.

"In second year, five of us, including Roy, decided to rent a house. The first month was unbelievable. You know how it is. You aren't far enough into the courses to have papers or mid-terms, so you party every night. Remember all the things I told you not to do at college? Well, I was speaking from experience.

"Then, one night in early October, Roy got a phone call saying his father had died of a heart attack. By the next afternoon he had dropped out of school and moved back to Port Huron.

"His father, a fine man, had a history of heart problems. He had worked in construction for only ten years when he had his first heart attack. The doctors told him not to go back to physical work, but unfortunately he wasn't qualified for much else. To his credit, he didn't give up. Instead, he trained to become a barber and eventually opened Miller's Barber Shop.

"Mrs. Miller worked as a maid during the day and as a waitress at night. Neither of them made a lot of money, but together they had enough to get by.

"When Mr. Miller died, Roy felt he had no choice but to quit school and go home to work. There was no way Mrs. Miller and Roy's younger sister, Ellen, could survive on a maid's pay. And, like so many people, Mr. Miller hadn't carried enough life insurance.

"During high school, Roy had become a pretty darn good barber himself. He had learned the tricks of the trade from hanging around his father's shop. When his dad was really busy, Roy would cut hair to help out. In fact, in our first year at college, he cut hair in residence to make some extra money.

"When Roy had to return home from the university, his game plan was simple. He was going to operate the barber shop until Ellen had completed college, and then he was going to sell it and go back to school. His sister was only in tenth grade at the time, so he was looking at about six years.

"We all felt bad about Roy having to put off his dream of becoming a lawyer, but deep down we knew he was doing the right thing. You've got to be there when your family needs you, even if it means personal sacrifice. You would do well to remember that, son, when your mother and I are old and want to move in with you."

"Don't even joke about that," I said in mock horror. "You still haven't explained how Roy became a financial planning expert. This isn't going to be one of your famous three-hour stories, is it?"

"No, no. I'm getting to the financial part.

"Roy did a tremendous job running the barber shop. He did some things that at the time were unique. Without a doubt, the most innovative and profitable was 'the hair truck.' Apart from the Tigers, Roy has always had two main hobbies. One is going to auctions and the other is tinkering with old cars and trucks. In his second year at the shop, he combined the two hobbies beautifully.

"He bought a barber chair at an auction and installed it in the back of an old moving truck. Then he put in a basin complete with running water, a power supply, and even a magazine rack. On Tuesdays, Roy took the hair truck to some of the local factories. He lifted the sliding door on the back and, voilà, he was open for business. The workers flocked over during their breaks and lunches. It was so convenient. What was the worst day of the week for most barbers was now Roy's best. In fact, he did so well on Tuesdays that he hired another barber to go back on Wednesdays and Thursdays. Eventually, a new ordinance put a stop to all the fun. But in the four or five years the hair truck was in operation, Roy brought in a lot of business and, more important, built a large and loyal clientele.

"He wasn't making a corporate lawyer's wage, but he was doing well . . . very well. We've never discussed what we make, but I would think our incomes over the years have been quite similar."

"What happened to the six-year plan?" I asked.

"Roy loved being a barber. It's as simple as that. To this day, he loves working downtown, dealing with people, owning his own business, all of it. It's funny, but Roy has really lived up to his most-likely-to-succeed billing. I don't know a more successful, well-rounded person."

"What about the financial planning part, Dad? I have to be home by Sunday, you know."

"I'm getting there. I'm getting there. Roy was really shaken by the poor financial shape his mother had been left in. His father had had no pension, no savings, and very little insurance. Roy laughs now when he says the only thing his father left them was a mortgage, but it wasn't funny at the time.

18

"He vowed not to make the same mistakes. Yet after a couple of years running the shop and making a good income, Roy had very little to show for his efforts. His mother and sister were being well taken care of, but financially, that was about it.

"Roy decided it was time to do something. He started reading everything he could on money management. At that time, almost all financial books concentrated on investment alternatives, not on mundane topics like saving, buying a house, and insurance—you know, the common person's concerns. They all showed what to do with money once you had it, but they didn't tell you how to accumulate it.

"However, Roy's father had always told him that if you want to learn to do something right, watch someone who does it successfully. Roy reasoned that that certainly held true for sports, so it probably held true for just about everything else, too, including financial planning.

"So, at the age of twenty-two, Roy did what he now calls the smartest thing he has ever done. He went to visit Maurice White.

"Old Mr. White was one of the wealthiest men in town. He owned a jewelry store, a huge farm, several race horses, and half the real estate downtown. Included in those holdings was the building that housed Miller's Barber Shop.

"Mr. White had always liked Roy. He admired him for his loyalty to his family and he was also impressed with Roy's entrepreneurial approach to increasing business. When Roy told Mr. White why he had dropped by, Mr. White nodded. 'You've come to the right place, my lad. I'll teach you *the golden secret* of financial success in one hour.'

"Well, David, that was quite an hour. I venture to say there aren't many barbers who started with nothing and today own a beautiful house on the lake, a large investment portfolio, an office building, and have their retirement well taken care of."

"All that from just one secret? What was it?" I asked eagerly.

"Slow down. It's not that simple. Roy continued to read and learn about financial planning. His knowledge of insurance, retirement plans, and investments has really helped him. But there's no doubt that hour was the catalyst. I'm not telling you any more, though. Roy teaches financial planning better than anyone, and I know he'll be more than happy to share his knowledge with you. In fact, I've already told him you won't be talking just about the Tigers tomorrow."

"I'm not sure I'll be able to follow him," I responded, feeling worried. "I don't understand all those fancy money terms, and as you may remember, math was never my strong suit."

"As I said earlier, son, it's just common sense. You'll be astonished when you learn how easy it is to handle your finances properly. If you listen to Roy, you'll never have any financial worries. You'll be so wealthy you'll be able to build your mother and me a guest house down in Ann Arbor."

"I'm not sure I want to be that wealthy," I said, slapping his shoulder affectionately.

* * *

"Boy, are you tanned!" I complimented Cathy, over breakfast. "It's only April and you're mahogany."

"Hanging out at the tanning studios?" Tom asked. "Man, that's an expensive habit. How much do those sessions cost?"

"Well, uh, I haven't been going to the studios. I bought my own tanning machine," an embarrassed Cathy replied.

"Must be nice! I slave all day at the plant to make ends meet and you're buying your own electric beach! If you'd just work on your personality a bit, I'd ask you to marry me."

"What if one of the girls you asked last night at the bar says yes? Bigamy is illegal, you know, Tom," Cathy pointed out.

"Oh, Tom," I groaned, "you weren't using that stale line again? What happened to, 'Excuse me, miss, can I buy you a Porsche?'"

"Gimme a break, you two. To meet women, a man's gotta do what a man's gotta do. Besides, that Porsche line has served me pretty well over the years."

"Well, I think it's running out of gas," Cathy teased. "Did you really buy a tanning machine, Sis?"

"Yeah. I had some extra money and I love being dark. Besides, it didn't cost all that much."

"I'll bet," I said sarcastically. "What do you do with all your money? You must own half of Port Huron by now."

"Hardly. With my car payments, mortgage payments, condo fees, credit cards, and daily living expenses, there's hardly anything left."

"Tough life, baby," Tom sighed. "You really should apply for some sort of government aid. SISIM or something —Supplemental Income for Single Independent Million-airesses."

"How can you party so hard at night and still be so witty in the morning, Tom? It never ceases to amaze me. Anyway, the truth is, I've blown my money pretty badly. Except for my down payment, my furnishings, and a small IRA, I haven't saved much at all. I get calls all the time from brokers and insurance agents who want to give me advice, but I distrust insurance agents, and I don't understand a thing brokers say."

"Talk about perfect timing. You won't believe the conversation I had with Dad last night! That's why I didn't go out. I wanted to discuss financial planning. With Sue and me about to have a baby, I want to start investigating things. We're looking for a house now. I'll need insurance . . . a college education fund for Davey Jr.—all that stuff."

"Davey Jr.? You must be kidding," Tom scoffed, between mouthfuls of his tenth piece of toast.

"So what did Dad say? I didn't know he knew anything about money."

"He didn't until six years ago. Then he learned the basics of financial planning and now he says he's in great shape. And you guys won't believe who taught him—Roy Miller."

"What the hell does Roy know about financial planning?" Tom demanded.

"A lot. You know how we figured Roy's wife must have inherited some pretty big money? Uh-uh. It turns out the house, the Lincoln, the boat—everything—were all earned through good financial planning. Roy started from scratch and with only average earnings turned himself into one wealthy barber."

"How?"

"I don't know yet, but you can bet I'm going to find out. In fact, our favorite barber is going to start teaching me this morning. Dad says Roy will tell me all I need to know to gain financial peace of mind."

"That sounds great. Do you two mind if I tag along today?" Cathy asked hopefully. "I don't need a shave—but I do need the advice."

"No, come on along," I invited her. "Who knows? Maybe one Saturday years from now, we'll be eating brunch on the Mediterranean, remembering this as the most important morning of our lives."

"The wealthy barber," Tom muttered, shaking his head.

Chapter 3

The Wealthy Barber

WHEN WE ARRIVED AT ROY'S, he was just finishing up Mr. Thacker's shave, if you can call it a shave. I don't think Mr. Thacker has had any facial hair growth since he turned ninety, five years ago.

"How are you, Johnny?" Mr. Thacker inquired, looking me straight in the eye.

"I'm Dave."

"Sorry, Dan. I always get you confused with your brother."

"I don't have a brother, Mr. Thacker. You're thinking of—"

"Dear me, what happened to your brother? The poor boy couldn't have been more than thirty!"

"I never had a brother. You're thinking of—"

"Oh, yes, I'm sorry. I thought you were one of the Richardson boys, the principal's sons."

I wasn't at all sure how to proceed at this point, but before I had a chance to decide, Mr. Thacker had started for the door.

"The old man's getting a bit senile, isn't he, Roy?" I sympathized, after the door had closed.

"Are you kidding, Davey? He knew who you were the whole time. It's all an act. He figures I won't ask him to pay if I think he's losing it."

"So, do you make him pay?" asked Tom.

"Sure do. If I gave a free cut to every weirdo who came in, I'd be broke in a month, and you two boys wouldn't have paid in years.

"Nice tan, Cathy!" Roy commented, before returning his attention to me. "Hey, Dave, did you see the article in the *Times Herald* last Wednesday on the female Midas here?"

Roy was referring to a full-page feature in the local paper that made my sister sound like the smartest and most talented woman alive.

"My mother showed it to me," I answered. "Five times."

"If you want to make it six, it's on the bottom of my birdcage," Tom added with a chuckle.

I myself didn't find that line particularly funny, but it got a couple of knee-slaps from Jimmy, who was reading the paper in the corner.

"Hey, where's Clyde?" I wondered.

"He's on vacation," James Murray informed me, "down in Florida at his sister's. I heard it was ninety-eight degrees down there yesterday. He'll be on a liquid diet for sure."

At this point I hopped up into Roy's chair. I always go before Tom, who insists on making sure Roy is warmed up before he'll go near him.

"I was talking to my father last night about financial planning. With Sue and me about to buy a house and have a baby, I figured it's time I learned a few things. Dad told me you know more about financial planning than anybody, so Cathy, Tom, and I are hoping you can teach us the basics."

"Your father mentioned on Thursday that he was going to recommend you talk to me. As I told him, I'd be more than happy to help out. He came to see me several years ago himself, and we put him on the right track."

"So I heard. That's good news. But he had some money to invest. I'm not sure you'll be able to do much for me. The only money Sue and I have is what we've saved for our down payment."

"Dave, investing and financial planning are not synonymous. Financial planning is really nothing more than the proper handling of cash flow and assets to meet your objectives. Oh, there are wills and insurance and a few other things, and we'll talk about all that later, but basically, how you handle your income and assets will determine your success.

"Let's be honest. Most young people don't have any assets, except maybe a home. So, it comes down to managing your cash flow."

"You mean budgeting?" I asked. "I'm terrible at that."

"No, I don't mean budgeting. Everybody's terrible at that. Very few people have become financially successful through budgeting, and the ones who have aren't much fun at parties."

"Ho, ho," Cathy piped up. "So, if we don't budget, how do we save money? I sure never have any left at the end of the month. I spend everything. The better business gets, the more I spend."

"Let's not get ahead of ourselves here. I admire your enthusiasm, but let's slow down a bit.

"I can make all three of you financially successful. I've done it for lots of people, these clowns included," Roy said, nodding at Jimmy and James. "Starting next month, each time you come in, I'll teach you a different part of a solid financial plan. Seven months from now, you'll be on the road to prosperity, and you'll tell everyone that Roy Miller is the greatest man who ever lived."

"We already tell people that, Roy," Tom said with a smile.

"How can you teach us so much in so little time? I mean, Roy, you really are working with novices. Tom and Dave and I are financial idiots!"

"Cathy, my job will be removing the word 'financial' from that statement. You'll have to worry about the other part yourselves. Trust me—good financial planning is nothing more than common sense. The old KISS philosophy at its best: Keep It Simple . . . Sweetheart.

"We all share pretty much the same goals—an annual vacation, a nice car, a comfortable home, early retirement, the ability to give our children what they need and want . . . and baseball season tickets. These are the average American's goals.

"And I'll tell you right now, they're easily attainable . . . easily. Especially if you start young. Time is your greatest ally. If you three start now, I guarantee you that you will exceed all your goals—dramatically.

"Look at me. I'm a barber, for crying out loud! I'm proud of my business, but I'm the first to admit that I'm not pulling in a doctor's salary. Far from it. Yet you'd be hard-pressed to find many professionals with better financial statements than mine. I hope it doesn't sound like I'm bragging. It's just that it's important for you to know that if someone as simple as me can become wealthy, it's certainly possible for you geniuses."

"You're not simple, Roy. Maybe a bit slow, but not simple," Tom wisecracked.

"I don't want to seem cynical, Roy, but if it's so easy, why isn't everyone doing it?" I asked.

"Lack of knowledge. Your dad and I talk about this all the time. Our schools don't teach money skills. Our family members don't talk money. And just as important, there are very few places an aspiring learner can turn to."

Tom looked quizzical. "What about financial planners?"

"Yes, there are many excellent financial planners. And when it comes to fine-tuning and implementing your plan they can be a great help. But when you're originally developing your plan, you must take responsibility for your own future. As I said earlier, the great thing is, it's not hard."

"Dad said last night that some old guy taught you a golden secret when you were young. What is it?" I probed.

"Oh, no. I'm saving that for next month. If you only pay attention once in the next seven months, let it be next month. If you follow that lesson, even if you do everything else poorly, I guarantee you that someday you'll be rich."

"Can't we start today?" I implored.

"No," Roy answered firmly. "My granddaughter's going to be here in five minutes. I'm taking care of her for the afternoon. Cathy can stay, but I want you two out of here ASAP. Emily's only three years old, and I don't want to scare her off men for the rest of her life."

Never before had I been tempted to get my hair cut two consecutive weeks. Roy had really piqued my interest. I've known him all my life and he has always come across as a very modest man. The matter-of-fact confidence he displayed when discussing Tom's, Cathy's, and my financial futures was out of character—and contagious. There was no doubt in my mind that I had taken the first step along the road to financial prosperity.

Chapter 4

The Ten Percent Solution

I CAN'T REMEMBER A RAINSTORM worse than the one that occurred on the third Saturday in May. A north wind had come up and was blowing at fifty miles an hour. That, combined with a torrential downpour, had caused most people to stay inside. Most smart people, that is.

There was no way Tom, Cathy, and I were going to miss out on the golden secret. We had been looking forward to it for a month. We were so excited, we even skipped breakfast at the Thomas Edison.

As usual, I drove. My parents' house has indoor access to the garage and both Tom and Cathy have underground parking so, surprisingly, it was possible to remain perfectly dry until we arrived at the shop. On the way there, Cathy suggested that Roy might be closed because of the weather. Tom and I just laughed. Roy hasn't missed an entire day of work in thirty-seven years for any reason. He had opened even on the morning of his daughter's wedding.

With so few people venturing out, we were able to get the parking spot right in front of Miller's. Between our umbrellas and his awning, we managed to get from the car to the shop door relatively unscathed.

28

It was locked.

Clyde, with his Florida tan, was standing on the other side peering out through the glass. "All you have to do is say, 'We love the Indians,' and I'll let you in. We've got coffee brewing," he chirped in his reedy voice.

By this time, we were starting to get pretty wet. And annoyed. The angle of the rain was such that it was impossible to protect ourselves completely, even with the help of the awning and umbrellas.

"I love the Indians!" Cathy cried, not amused.

Traitor. Tom and I stood stoically.

Clyde shook his head and let all of us in. "You boys really are die-hards. You should seek professional help."

"You telling us we need a psychiatrist is like Karl Malden telling someone he needs a nose job," Tom murmured, as he toweled off.

"I thought you three might not show. It's terrible out there," Roy commented.

"What? And miss our long-awaited, eagerly anticipated first lesson? You've got to be kidding!" I retorted. "What I can't believe is that these three have shown up in this weather," I added, motioning toward Clyde, Jimmy, and James Murray. I'm not sure why I always use James Murray's given and family names. Perhaps it's because, when I was young, I thought his name was James-Murray, like Billy-Bob or Bobby-Joe.

"They wouldn't miss free coffee and doughnuts if we had a tornado. You should know that by now," Roy replied, as he straightened up the counter.

"Roy, I've been looking forward to today for a month. My financial situation is getting worse instead of better," Cathy began impatiently. "I can hardly wait to hear what you have to say."

"OK, let's get started. As your father has probably told you, I took over this shop thirty-odd years ago when my dad died. I got lucky and a few of my ideas paid off. After a couple of years, I was making a pretty good income. Very good for a barber. I added a couple of chairs in the other room and, all in all, things were moving along well.

"I decided to make barbering my life's work. I knew my income from the shop was respectable, but it was never going to make me a rich man. That bothered me because, frankly, I wanted to be wealthy. I grew up poor and, believe me, it's something you don't acquire a taste for. I didn't want to live in town in a tiny, one-bedroom home—I wanted to live on the lake. I wanted to own this building, too. I wanted a nice car, trips to Europe, and some of the other fine things life has to offer.

"The only way I could accomplish all that on my income was to budget and save like a madman. Or, at least, that's what I thought. So, I developed a budget: so much for rent, so much for food, so much for clothes, so much for savings . . . you know. Two years after starting to budget, I had very little to show for it. Sure enough, at the end of each month I'd end up saying, 'So much for savings,' but, unfortunately, it didn't mean what I had hoped it would mean. It was pretty depressing.

"Like you, Dave, I realized I didn't know anything about financial planning, and it was high time to learn. I didn't have a father to turn to, so I went to a person who I figured must know a lot about money, he had so much— Old Mr. White.

"I explained my situation to him. I told him what I wanted to achieve. 'Is it possible?' I asked.

"He told me, 'Wealth beyond your wildest dreams is possible if you follow the golden rule: Invest ten percent of all you make for long-term growth. If you follow that one simple guideline, someday you'll be a very rich man.'"

"That's it?" asked Tom, making no attempt to hide his disappointment.

"Patience, Tom," replied Roy. "Patience. I felt the same way myself. I wasn't very impressed when Mr. White told me, either. My budget was already designed to save even more than ten percent and, at that point, it wasn't working and I was far from wealthy. But Mr. White went on to explain a few things that I'll tell you now . . . things that turn a seemingly simple sentence into an extremely powerful thought.

"Cathy, if you invested twenty-four hundred dollars a year, say two hundred dollars a month, for the next thirty years, and averaged a fifteen percent return a year, how much money do you think you'd end up with?" Roy challenged.

"Well, twenty-four hundred times thirty is . . . seventy-two thousand—"

"I'm impressed," I interrupted.

"Plus growth . . . I don't know . . . I'd say two hundred thousand. Maybe not quite that much," Cathy concluded.

"Wrong. The answer is one point four million dollars," Roy declared.

"Get real!" was Tom's initial reaction. When he realized that Roy was serious, he paled. "What about inflation? And where am I going to get fifteen percent? For that matter, where am I going to get two hundred dollars a month?" he stammered.

"All good questions, Tom, and we'll get to them in due course. Dave, you try one. If you had started putting thirty dollars a month away, the equivalent of a dollar a day, at age eighteen and you continued until age sixty-five, averaging a fifteen percent annual return, how much would you end up with?"

"I hate math, Roy, but I'll give it a shot. Thirty dollars a month is three hundred and sixty dollars a year, times forty-seven years . . . Anybody have a calculator?"

"It's just under seventeen thousand," Roy interjected.

"Plus growth. I'll say around seventy thousand."

"Close," Roy responded. "The answer is two million six hundred and seventy-nine thousand dollars."

"Bull," Tom scoffed, as if he had read my mind.

"No, not bull . . . magic. The magic of compound interest. The eighth wonder of the world. Thirty dollars a month, a dollar a day, will magically turn into over two

31

and a half million. And do you know what's even more impressive? You know someone who has done it," Roy said proudly.

"Thirty-five years ago, I started my savings with thirty dollars a month, which was approximately ten percent of my earnings. I have achieved just under a fifteen percent average annual return. In addition, as my income rose, my ten percent saving component rose accordingly. Thirty dollars a month became sixty dollars, then a hundred, and eventually hundreds of dollars a month.

"You three are looking at a very wealthy man."

"Are you trying to tell us that, by saving ten percent of every paycheck, you've turned yourself into a millionaire?" an intense Tom demanded.

"Precisely," was the incredible response.

Roy Miller, a millionaire! I sat stunned. I knew he had done well, but a millionaire? To the best of my knowledge, I'd never met a millionaire, and I sure didn't expect my first to be my barber. Roy was clearly deriving great pleasure from the disbelief on our three faces.

"Compound interest . . . mind-boggling, isn't it?" he went on. "When the Indians sold Manhattan to the Dutch for beads worth twenty-four dollars, it seemed that the natives got taken. But if they had invested that money at eight percent interest, today their investment would be worth trillions of dollars."

"Have you ever thought about buying Manhattan, Roy?" Cathy teased.

"It's a real tragedy that most people don't understand compound interest and its wondrous powers. Take your dad, Dave. If he had started his program at the same time I did, you'd be looking at a big inheritance down the road."

"You still haven't answered my questions about the effects of inflation, where we get fifteen percent, and how we save two hundred a month," Tom said. "Hell, I'm lucky to save two hundred a year and, even if I could save money, I don't know anything about investing—the stock market, options, commodities . . . C'mon, Roy, you've got to be kidding!''

Tom's points were well taken. Saving money is never easy. No one—and I mean no one—has devoted more time to developing a budget than Susan and I. Yet every month, apart from our down-payment fund, we don't manage to save a cent. As for investing, the only investment I've ever made was in a penny stock. I lost six hundred dollars in one week. Six hundred dollars I couldn't afford to lose. Six hundred dollars that was needed for my tuition.

''I'll talk about saving and investing in a minute,'' Roy commenced. ''As for inflation, well, I'm sure that, in the mid-fifties, people probably said, 'Yeah, saving ten per-cent sounds like a good idea, but what's a million going to be worth in the nineties, anyway?' Sure, inflation is go-ing to have an impact. But not a devastating one. Far from it. In fact, inflation is all the more reason to save. Things are going to get more expensive. Lakefront properties are going to continue to rise in price. Lincolns are going to cost more. But, believe me, if you save ten percent, you'll be parking your Continental beside your vacation home someday. Remember that your wages will continue to rise too, as will your ten percent saving. My original ten per-cent stake was only thirty dollars a month; yours will be much more, and so will your total wealth. That will do a lot to offset inflation. If you handle your savings wisely, your growth rate should far exceed the inflation rate. Maybe not every year, but certainly on average.

''It's the person who doesn't save ten percent who has to worry about inflation, not the person who does,'' he summarized.

''So how do we earn fif—''

''Slow down, slow down. Let's talk about saving the money first. When people think about saving, they think about budgeting. I'll allot so much of my income for this, so much for that, et cetera, et cetera, and at the end of the month, I'll have so much left over. But as each of us knows all too well, something goes wrong. Money keeps running out before the month does.

"You know, it's funny. When I took over the shop, it was obvious that cost management hadn't been one of my father's strengths. I designed a detailed budget that covered all my potential expenses. I stuck to it like glue. That budget played a major part in my early success. To this day, I still do a shop budget once a year. And I still stick to it.

"After a couple of years running the shop, I couldn't understand how my personal budget could be such a waste of time, while my business budget worked like a charm. I discussed the situation with Old Mr. White. I'll never forget his reply. 'Roy, my young friend,' he said, 'a business only has to budget for needs. It's in the best interest of the business to limit those needs as much as possible. An individual, on the other hand, must budget for both needs and wants. It is a rare person who can do that success-fully because, for too many people, *a want becomes a need.*'

"And it's so true! Did I need a new car in my second year of business, or did I just want one? Cathy, did you need to get away to Europe last winter, or did you just want to? Tom, did you need, or just want, the best stereo available? It's human nature to spend our entire disposable income and to rationalize all those expenditures as needs."

"Good point, Roy, but you have to have some fun, too. One of the reasons I make money is to spend it on things I like," I argued.

"Young people of all generations think alike, Dave. That's exactly what I said to Mr. White. Remember, I grew up poor. My first couple of years at the shop was the first time I'd ever had any fun money. 'No one is trying to tell you to squirrel away every cent, Roy,' Mr. White explained. 'But if you want to accomplish your goals, you must save something. I think you can see that. Luckily, there is an almost painless way to save—a way to save where you barely notice the money is gone!'"

"I might not know much about financial matters," Tom blurted out, "but I know there's no painless way to save . . . no way, no how."

A voice sounded from the corner of the room. "Be quiet and listen."

The source of that remark really caught me off guard. In the over twenty years I had known him, Clyde had not said one serious thing. And that's not an exaggeration. That he was even paying attention to such a no-nonsense conversation was startling, let alone that he seemed eager for it to continue.

"Clyde," Roy asked mischievously, "is there a painless way to save?"

"Sure is. Pay yourself first. Old Mr. White knew what he was talking about when he told you that." Clyde nodded.

"Oh, no," Tom muttered. "The wealthy barber I can take, but the wealthy wacko . . . that's too much!"

Roy and Clyde just grinned at each other.

"Pay yourself first. I can't tell you what those three little words have meant to me," Roy reflected. "After agreeing that the ad hoc approach to saving doesn't work, and after explaining to me why the budgeting approach seldom works, Mr. White announced that the only way to save is to pay yourself first. Although he was talking about saving the ten percent, the axiom holds true for all savings. Whether you're saving for a down payment, a car, a trip, whatever, the most effective thing is to have the money come right off your paycheck, or right out of your bank—*before you have a chance to spend it.* But we'll talk more about saving for those kinds of items in a few months.

"Anyway, I was a bit skeptical at first. I was helping my mom and sister get by, paying my shop's rent, making car payments, and trying to save for both a down payment and an engagement ring. And I wasn't meeting with much success. In my mind, there was no way I could set aside an additional ten percent. Where was I going to get that thirty dollars a month? There was nothing left at the end of the month as it was. I had tried budgeting and that hadn't worked. Then Mr. White made a very generous offer. 'Roy, you arrange to have that thirty dollars a month go directly into a separate bank account, and from there to an investment. If at any time saving that thirty dollars runs you short of funds, I'll lend you whatever you need at no interest. You can pay me back whenever it's convenient for you.'

"How could I say no? Anyway, I never did miss that money. My lifestyle didn't change at all. I know thirty dollars doesn't sound like much now, but remember, it was ten percent of my income back then, and I never missed it.

"But the best example I've ever seen of the pay-yourself-first rule not adversely affecting someone's life is Clyde.

"Good pension at work, lived in an apartment, no wife, no kids, no debt—that was Clyde fifteen years ago. Actually, that's Clyde today, too. In the mid-seventies, Clyde told me he had his eye on a gorgeous twenty-thousand-dollar sailboat that he'd love to have for his 'retirement home.' You could get a heck of a boat back then for twenty grand. I reminded Clyde, though, that by the time he retired in '95 or so, thanks to inflation that boat would cost a pretty penny more. The only way he would be able to afford it would be to start putting aside money right away. We started him on a couple of hundred a month—a very big chunk of his income back then. 'I'll never survive,'" Roy mimicked. "'I won't be able to go out at all. I'll have to go Dutch on my dates.'

"Clyde was convinced bankruptcy was just around the corner. Four months after we started the saving program, I asked him how he was struggling along without the two hundred dollars a month. He said, 'Geez, I'd forgotten all about that.'

"The significance of that reply can't be overstated. He'd forgotten he was even doing it! Over the years I've taught dozens of people the pay-yourself-ten-percent-first rule. Not one has noticed a dramatic change in his or her standard of living . . . until they're sipping martinis on their boats, that is,'' Roy reported, with a satisfied grin.

"Ask your dad, Dave. He'll tell you. It really is amazing. You know how quickly you adjust to your raises? Well, this is pretty much the same thing, but in reverse.''

"I don't make a lot of money and I didn't start saving until fifteen years ago. But today I'm not only looking at a boat; I'm looking at a pretty darn good retirement overall. If you three start at your age, the sky's the limit,'' Clyde beamed, as he gave Tom an encouraging pat on the back.

"I want to make something clear here,'' Roy proceeded. "At different times in your life, you're going to have to save for various things—a house, a car, a trip, whatever. A house, in particular, is a major expenditure. There is no way to achieve some goals without sacrificing your current standard of living . . . I mean, let's be realistic. But the ten percent saving is different. It's regular. It's a constant. You don't even see it. It comes right off your paycheck or out of your bank. You won't believe how easy that makes it.''

"I can see that saving ten percent of your income shouldn't be too hard, especially if you pay yourself first. But I'm still curious about those fifteen percent rates of return,'' Tom persisted. "Last time I looked at my savings, which I admit are pitiful, they were earning a paltry five percent.''

"Achieving higher rates of return over the long run is simple,'' Roy shrugged. "Be an owner, not a loaner.''

"C'mon, Roy, I don't know anything about owning stocks or gold or real estate,'' Tom protested. "Hell, I saw what the market did in October '87. I want no part of that.''

"Tom, you missed four key words—'over the long run.' Ownership, at least ownership governed by common sense, will always outperform loaning in the long run. It has to.

If it's consistently more profitable for businesses and individuals to leave their money in the bank than to invest it in North American enterprises, we're all in big trouble. Eventually, our whole economic system would collapse. That isn't going to happen. And in the unlikely event that it did, it wouldn't do you any good to have your money sitting down at the bank . . . because the banks would all be locked,'' Roy laughed.

"You see, despite all the bitching and complaining and all the predictions of doom and gloom, times are good and, again I emphasize 'over the long run,' they'll continue to get better. VCRs, microwaves, gas barbecues . . . your parents didn't enjoy perks like that when they were young. Technological advances, medical discoveries, social programs . . . do I have to go on? The fact is, we're living in great times. If you're healthy and living in the United States, guys like you have very little to complain about, apart from the Tiger pitching staff.

"I know we've got huge deficits, major environmental problems, several social ills, and so on. And these are serious problems. Unfortunately, we'll always have serious problems. However, equating 'serious' with 'fatal' would be to greatly underestimate this country. 'It is a gloomy moment in history . . . never has the future seemed so dark and incalculable. The United States is beset with racial, industrial and commercial chaos, drifting we know not where. Of our troubles, no man can see the end.'

"Quite an editorial, don't you think? It was written in *Harper's Magazine*. Do you know when? 1847! I think you get my point.

"I believe that the next twenty to thirty years will present some of the greatest opportunities ever. So much change. So many things happening. The only way to be a part of it all and to share in the successes is through ownership."

"So, should we buy common stocks?" I asked.

"No, with your ten percent savings, common stocks are not the way to go," was Roy's solemn warning.

Needless to say, this caught me by surprise. "You've never owned a common stock?" I questioned.

"Never. I don't know anything about stock analysis, and I don't have any friends who do, either. It's a tough game. You have to be disciplined. To perform well, you have to buy when everyone else is selling and sell when everyone else is buying, a rare combination of guts and brains. You have to have a good background in economics and you have to use that background to look into the future. You not only have to see the various companies' management teams, you have to know what questions to ask them. Most of all, you have to have a sixth sense, an intuition, a knack of recognizing value. Very few people fill the bill. I certainly don't. I mean, think about it. Do you know anybody who's become rich buying and selling stocks? There aren't many. It's just too difficult."

"What about using stockbrokers? They must know what they're doing," I asserted.

"I was a stockbroker for several years, Dave," James Murray noted, "and I can assure you that, when it comes to picking and choosing stocks, a broker is usually no better than the next guy."

"They're around stocks all day; they must know something."

"Dave, most are salespeople. That's it. Instead of selling shoes or beds, they're selling stocks. They spend all day on the phone talking to clients, reading research reports, looking at undecipherable financial statements. In the five years I was a broker, only one guy in our office turned a profit in his personal trading account in any calendar year. One!"

"You?"

"Me? I was the worst! I thought I was a hotshot because I was driving a fancy car, eating at pricey restaurants, and taking home a hefty check. Unfortunately, I couldn't have consistently picked winning stocks if my life had depended on it.

"After seven years, I got disgusted and quit. My commissions were great but my clients' investment performance was dismal. It hit me hard when I realized it's all a game. You know what still bothers me? Most of my clients were really happy with me. I gave excellent service, was nice on the phone, threw good cocktail parties, and knew all the right things to say. I know I could have remained a prosperous broker for years, losing people's money the whole time.

"One guy in our office was nearing retirement when I came aboard. He'd been a broker for thirty years, and was very well thought of. When he retired to his summer home and yacht, his accounts were divvied up. I got ninety of them, some very good. I started examining what he had been doing for the clients so I'd be well informed when I called to introduce myself. I'll never forget it. Of ninety accounts, only seven were up money over the years, and only one of those was up dramatically."

"Why do people stay with their brokers if they constantly lose money?" Cathy inquired.

"Who knows? Some don't stay. They switch to other brokers, who often also end up losing them money. Others don't care, because they play the market for excitement more than profit. And I know this sounds hard to believe, but I'm convinced that many don't even know whether they're up or down.

"I remember one client who had been dealing with the retiring broker for fifteen years. He had started with fifty thousand and, fifteen years later, he had fifty-five thousand. 'That's better than a loss,' he said. He didn't understand that if he had just left the money in the bank, he would have had substantially more than fifty-five thousand. Like so many others, he didn't understand compound interest.

"A major reason people lose money with their brokers is that they constantly go against the wisdom of *let your profits run and cut your losses.* Most investors and brokers cut profits and let losses run.

"Good investors admit their mistakes and sell, taking small losses. Those losses are easily covered by the large profits created through a combination of buying value and exercising patience . . . patience that most of us don't have.

"Bad investors always think their stocks are going to come back up to at least what they cost them. Brokers know they look bad when they choose a loser so, rather than selling and accepting a loss, they perpetuate this myth. A stock doesn't know you own it—it's not going back to twenty-two so you can get out even. So, you often end up holding as the stock goes lower and lower."

"James, are you saying brokers are dishonest?" Cathy probed.

"No, no . . . I didn't mean it that way. I think reluctance to admit a mistake is human nature, not deliberate dishonesty. Sometimes we can't even admit to ourselves that we were wrong.

"I'd say ninety percent of the brokers I have known are professional and honest.

"The press is constantly alleging that brokers *churn* accounts, meaning they trade them excessively to generate commissions. I saw very little of that while I was a broker. For the most part, I don't think that brokers' poor investment performance has anything to do with ethics. Picking stocks successfully is very difficult, and most of us just aren't capable of doing it. It's as simple as that. And, like I said earlier, most brokers are salespeople, not investment advisors. The bottom line is, if brokers were really so smart, they wouldn't need clients."

"So, we should never use a broker," Tom summarized.

"We didn't say that," Roy clarified. "We said you shouldn't invest your ten percent fund in common stocks on your own or with help from a broker. But there are a lot of fine brokers out there and, used properly, they can be a big help in achieving financial success."

"But what else does a broker do?" I asked.

"Many stockbrokers no longer specialize in stock trading but instead now concentrate on offering to their clients a more well-rounded financial planning service involving many of the products and concepts that we'll be discussing over the next several months."

"You want us to invest in ownership but not in common stocks. I guess that leaves real estate. What should we do? Buy a square foot each month with our two hundred dollars?"

Obviously, Tom was kidding, but I thought he had asked a fairly good question. Is there such a thing as a two-hundred-dollar parcel of land?

"Real estate is a very real possibility," Roy acknowledged. "Not by buying a square foot a month, mind you. We'll get into that later, too. First, let's look at what I think is the best alternative for investing the ten percent, at least for people who won't need the money for years: equity-oriented mutual funds."

I frowned. "I thought the stock market was a losing game. Don't equity-oriented mutual funds own primarily common stock?"

"I've read some bad things about mutual funds lately," Cathy said. "A lot of people lost big money in mutuals during the crash, didn't they?"

"I didn't say the stock market is a losing game. I said buying and selling stocks on your own or on your broker's advice is usually a losing game. The stock market has actually been very good to investors who have the qualities we spoke of earlier: intelligence, courage, patience, and an eye for value," Roy replied.

"A carefully selected mutual fund gives you access to a professional money manager who demonstrates those qualities. You won't be making the individual investment decisions. A professional will.

"Simply stated, a mutual fund is a professionally managed pool of money. The pool is made up of money from people like you and me, people numbering in the thousands. We all put our money together and hand it over to someone who knows, or supposedly knows, what he or she is doing.

"There are all sorts of benefits. Most important is the one I just mentioned: professional money management. Second, mutuals give you diversification. Most people don't have enough money to buy a properly diversified portfolio, with stocks in different industries in a variety of countries. By pooling resources, individuals can gain a pro-rata share in a vast array of securities. 'Don't put all your eggs in one basket,' and all that stuff. Third, mutual funds are a *hands off* investment. There is no on-going research and decision-making process required of the investor. This feature is very important. Most of us don't have time to look after our investments. We work all day. With mutual funds, that isn't a problem. They have a low PITA factor."

"What's a PITA factor?"

"Pain In The Ass factor . . . a highly technical investment term." Roy chuckled.

"You make mutual funds sound perfect. If they're so great, why do they seem to get a fair amount of bad press?" Cathy challenged.

"Oh, they're far from perfect. Like all equity vehicles, that is, investments involving ownership, they are subject to risk. There are no guarantees, and they do fluctuate up and down. If the market takes a steep fall, your mutual fund will likely tumble with it. If your professional money manager makes a series of bad investment decisions, they will be reflected in the performance of the fund, no doubt about it.

"And always bear this in mind: If you buy a common-stock fund at the height of the market, you're asking for trouble. 'Buy low, sell high' has long been a cliché of the investment business, but truer words have never been spoken. If you rush in and buy a fund, or for that matter any investment, because your neighbor's has tripled in the last five years, you're probably making a mistake. It's when your neighbor's investment has gone down thirty percent over the last two years that you're probably looking at a good time to buy.

"In addition to the fact that it's hard to time your purchase, and that mutual funds are subject to market fluctuations, there are a couple of other drawbacks.

"Mutual funds are very long-term investments. Precisely because they are hard to time and they do fluctuate, an investor has to be thinking long-term. Over a period of, say, seven to ten years, the economy, and therefore the market, will most likely continue to spiral upward. If you're willing to hold your fund for that length of time, you'll have little to worry about. But if you're buying a fund for a two- or three-year period, you'd better be a lot smarter than me! I'm confident that the market will perform well over the long run. It always has. But I'm not sure where it's going over the next couple of years. As I've gotten older, I've realized no one else is, either. No one. As for consistently accurate short-term forecasters, there is no such animal.

"One final problem with mutual funds: They're boring. Nobody goes to a party and talks about how their mutual fund went up two cents yesterday. Individual stocks, real estate, options, commodities, these all carry an aura of excitement . . . a bit of Vegas. Not funds. Nobody's ever called mutual funds an exciting way to invest your money."

"That seems like a lot of problems for what you termed our 'best alternative,'" I pointed out.

"It may seem that way, Dave, but when you examine it closely, it isn't that way at all. I'll prove it, one 'problem' at a time.

"First, market fluctuations. Like a roller coaster, they're fun on the way up, and scary on the way down. But, thanks to the power of *dollar cost averaging,* even downside fluctuations can work to your advantage.

"Dollar cost averaging is as close to infallible investing as you can get. It genuinely slants the odds in an investor's favor, yet I've read all kinds of financial planning books that haven't even mentioned it. Most people haven't even heard of it."

"I haven't," Cathy admitted. "Is it hard to do?"

"It's as easy as pie," Roy assured her. "The technical definition is, 'A system of buying common stocks or mutual fund shares at regular intervals with a fixed dollar amount.' Whoop-de-do, you say?

"Let's see how something that sounds so theoretical can easily produce fantastic results.

"Tom, say you decide to save one hundred dollars a month and invest it in fund XYZ. The month you start your program, XYZ is trading at ten dollars a share so, obviously, you buy ten shares. The second month XYZ has dropped by fifty percent, all the way to five dollars . . . not good. Your hundred dollars now buys you twenty shares. In month three, the fund has rebounded somewhat and now trades at seven dollars and fifty cents, still well under your original purchase price. You buy thirteen and a third shares. So, what's happened?"

"I've lost money following your advice. That's what happened," Tom answered.

"No, you haven't," I interrupted confidently. "You've broken even. You're down two-fifty a share on your purchase at ten, you're up two-fifty a share on your purchase at five, and you're even on your final purchase."

Roy corrected us. "You're both wrong."

"I hate math," I growled. "But how can I be wrong? It's just a question of average price. Even I can figure out the average of three numbers."

"How many shares does Tom own?" Roy asked. He then quickly answered his own question, "Forty-three and a third. And how much are the shares currently worth? Seven dollars and fifty cents each. What's forty-three and a third times seven-fifty? Three hundred and twenty-five. How much had Tom invested? Three hundred. He's up twenty-five dollars, an excellent return over such a short period of time."

"How the—"

"Because you're putting in a fixed amount each month, you obtain more shares at the lower prices. You bought twenty shares at five, but only ten at ten. Basically, it means that your average cost per share will be lower than the average price per share. In the long run, or even in the short run, that bodes well for the investor.

"So, one month when the stock market is struggling and your mutual fund is suffering accordingly, don't look at the situation and say, 'Darn, my holding is down.' Look at it and say, 'Eventually the market will go up and take the value of my holding with it, so in the meantime I'm going to pick up shares at a good price.' Dollar cost averaging is great stuff!

"With mutuals, problem number two is timing. It's very difficult for an amateur, or even a professional, to time a purchase accurately. Well, it's no problem at all when you buy monthly. We're not buying once; we're buying continually. Sometimes we'll buy high; but sometimes we'll buy low. When the market goes into a prolonged slump, there we are, picking up shares at good prices, month after month. Forget discipline, courage, intelligence, and an eye for value. We don't need any of them. We buy every month.

"Does a steep decline like Black Monday hurt our holdings? Sure it does. But the market will bounce back. It always has. And while it's down, we're picking shares up at rock-bottom prices—a lot of shares, thanks to dollar cost averaging."

"I guess the fact that mutual funds are long-term investments isn't a problem either," Cathy mused. "We're going to be accumulating and holding shares for ten, twenty, maybe even thirty years. We are the consummate long-term investors. As you said, short-term downturns, even prolonged downturns, will work to our advantage, not to our detriment. This sounds great, Roy!"

"It *is* great, Cathy. And as far as mutual funds not being a glamorous investment, well, so what? After they've earned you good returns, you can use the profits to buy more exciting things if you want . . . such as the satellite dish I bought yesterday."

"Get out! Dave and I will be over tomorrow to watch the Tigers game. Put a few on ice, will you, Roy?"

"I love you guys like sons, but if you ever come near my house, I'll call the police."

"Some father you must be," Tom pouted.

An intrigued Cathy pressed on. "What mutual funds should we buy, Roy, and how do we purchase them?"

"Good questions. I'm going to leave it to the three of you to select your own funds, but let me give you a few pointers.

"Too often, mutual funds are discussed in blanket terms. 'I don't like mutual funds.' 'I heard about someone who made a killing in mutual funds.' That type of thing. But all mutual funds are not created equal. Some I like; some I don't.

"The key is the manager. You're buying professional money management and there can be as big a difference between two professional money managers as there can be between two professional quarterbacks. If I asked you, 'Who do you want on your team, Bob Gagliano or Joe Montana?' I feel certain you'd all answer the latter. When you're selecting a fund, find the Montana of money management."

"How do we do that?"

"If you were assigned to select the best QB in the NFL but didn't follow football, where would you start? You'd look at statistics, of course. Who is the highest-rated passer? Who's the most consistent? Has he been good for just one year, or has he proven he can do it year after year? When times are tough and his team is struggling, does he maintain a high level of play, or drop off badly? Once you had studied the statistics, you would read some articles and talk to people in the know. What are the experts' opinions? Do they jibe with your findings?

"It's no different when you're looking for a good mutual fund. Assess past records. They don't guarantee future results, but they sure as heck are a good indication of the manager's abilities. What's the five-year average return? Ten-year? Fifteen-year? Does the fund perform consistently, or is it way up one year and way down the next? How does it fare during the bad times? Some funds have excellent records during tough times.

"Do some reading! *Money* and *Forbes* magazines do tremendous jobs monitoring mutual fund performance and highlighting industry leaders. In fact, once a year, both of these fine periodicals have in-depth mutual fund summary charts that include average return figures over various lengths of time, ratings for performance during both good times and bad, commission charges, and pretty much everything else you could possibly want to know."

"Can't you give us any other tips, Roy?" Cathy pleaded. "We need all the help we can get!"

"For you, anything. OK. Point one: Make sure that if a fund has solid rates of return, the manager who created them is still there. You're not buying past performance numbers; you're buying a manager's expertise. If fund ABC averaged fifteen percent a year under the guidance of Jack Smith, but Jack Smith has left, stay away from ABC. You can't be sure what you're getting.

"Two: Buy a global fund that invests across many different industries. You don't want to buy a fund that invests in only one country or in only one industry—that's poor diversification. Give the manager as much flexibility as possible to invest wherever he or she sees fit. Oh, by the way, don't confuse the terms 'international fund' and 'global fund.' An international fund invests solely in foreign securities. Omitting the U.S. from investment considerations would be a big mistake! Global funds invest in both foreign and U.S. securities.

"Three: Avoid the currently-very-popular market-timing schemes and sector-fund-switching concepts," Roy cautioned.

"Cool it, Roy," interjected Tom, using his usual direct style to express his confusion.

"Not familiar with those terms, Tom?" Roy chuckled. "Good thing, because, frankly, neither of them works anyway. Market timing is just what it sounds like. By using certain key indicators, such as recent interest-rate movements, you or your 'guru' attempt to time major market movements and shift your money from one type of fund to another accordingly. For instance, when the indicators point to a market decline you're instructed to move your money to the safe haven of a money-market fund and away from the soon-to-fall stock market. Conversely, when an interest rate decline is sensed, back to the market you go just in time to catch the predicted rebound. In theory this sounds great, but in practice it seldom works. The various indicators, at best, can be termed unreliable, or perhaps more important, it is our ability to select and evaluate the proper indicators that is unreliable. The advocates of market timing dispute this and offer proof of their wisdom through back-tested models. 'If you had followed our formula, here's how you would have fared over the last twenty years.' They never mention that the reason you would have fared that well is that the system they're offering was back-tested so thoroughly that it, in essence, was indeed *developed* to yield good performance figures over the last twenty years!

"Even if developing a consistent, accurate market-timing formula was really possible, it wouldn't be sustainable for the simple reason that the market operates on a divergence of opinions—those of buyers and those of sellers. Accurate and consistent market timing would eliminate that divergence. To tell the truth, I think it's somewhat silly that market timing gets as much attention as it does when you consider the actual, not the back-tested, but the actual track record of its proponents.

"Sector-fund switching works in a similar fashion to market timing. On the advice of an expert, usually self-proclaimed, you move from a mutual fund investing in an industry about to decline to a mutual fund that invests in one about to rise, thereby always catching the major upswings in the various industries."

"Even I can see the unlikelihood of someone possessing that kind of ability. If someone really was that smart, why would he or she need or want to share the information with me?" Cathy reasoned soundly.

"Good point," Roy said, smiling, "very good point. The experiences of the few people I've known who have tried sector timing have been so bad as to almost be funny. Instead of switching at the opportune moment, they've switched from one sector fund when they've become frustrated with its poor performance—sold low—into another sector fund that has boasted a much better recent track record—bought high."

"You know, using sector funds also tends to eliminate one of the major advantages of mutual funds that you mentioned earlier—diversification," I added proudly.

"Yes, I do know," Roy agreed with a wink. "With your ten percent solution, stick to a global fund whose manager emphasizes value and growth potential, not one whose manager chases fads or tries to be wherever the action is. Find one who uses common sense, discipline, and patience to select and hold stocks that offer good value; stocks that, at the time of purchase, others are overlooking. This is key!

"Four: Watch your commissions. The fund I used had a high commission structure, but it has been well worth the cost. Nonetheless, it's certainly in your best interest to limit your commission, or load, as it is frequently called. That load is sometimes as high as eight and a half percent, so that for every dollar you put in, eight and a half cents come right off the top—obviously not ideal. Because of that, many financial experts recommend buying only no-load funds, adding that there are scores of excellent ones available. For the most part, I agree with that advice but, as with every rule, there are a couple of exceptions. If you need the help of a stockbroker, mutual fund salesperson, insurance agent, or financial planner in selecting a fund, obviously you should pay for that help. Frankly, their expertise can make it worth paying the load, especially if you are unable or unwilling to do the necessary homework yourself. A second exception can occur if you, after doing your own research, are convinced that the best fund for you is a load-fund. Turning your back on an excellent fund, especially one that you feel comfortable with, just because there's a commission makes little sense."

"I'm a little perplexed," Cathy admitted. "If the load in a load fund goes to your advisor or salesperson, how does the actual manager of such a fund make money?"

"In addition to a potential load there is always, I repeat always, a management fee. Nobody works for free nor, for that matter, should be asked to. In addition to the fund manager's fee, certain other charges are often apportioned to the fund's shareholders. These charges may include everything from accounting fees to the cost of mailing reports. These—"

"Whoa, whoa, whoa there," Tom interrupted Roy. "Isn't all that going to get a little heavy?"

"Actually, it's not as expensive as you'd think. The expense ratio—all of the management fees and costs lumped together and expressed as a percentage of the total fund value—is often as low as one percent and seldom higher than two percent," Roy countered.

"Yeah, but if my fund shows an average annual return of fifteen percent, that two percent is going to knock it down to thirteen—that hurts," Tom pushed on.

"The two percent expense ratio you refer to in your example, Tom, is already reflected in the fund's reported fifteen percent average annual return. So—"

"Well, then, what the heck do I care what the expense ratio is?" Again Tom cut Roy off. "If it's too high, that is, if the managers are charging more than they're worth, that will be reflected in the past-performance figures."

Makes sense, I thought.

"True," Roy somewhat reluctantly agreed, "but I have two caveats. One: Make sure the current expense ratio is

51

in line with the past expense ratios, or past performance numbers may be difficult to sustain. Two: All else being equal, including the past performance records, I'd rather buy the fund with the lower expense ratio because I believe it may be easier for them to maintain that performance.''

"But the other fund must have slightly better managers, though, and so—"

"Shut up, Tom," Roy said, diplomatically closing off our discussion of expense ratios.

"Any more points, Roy?" Cathy pressed on amid the laughter.

"Stay away from mutual funds that use complicated strategies. Generally speaking, the trickier the fund, the lower the returns. Option funds, future funds, hedge funds—they all have two things in common: They sound sophisticated and they usually underperform. Remember, value and growth, they're the keys. Find a fund manager who emphasizes sound and simple principles. That's the ticket!

"Finally, I want to re-emphasize the importance of a good long-term track record. Anybody can get hot for a few years, but if someone has had superior rates of return for a fifteen- or twenty-year period, that's a good indication that he knows what he's doing . . . Oops, sorry, Cathy.

"As for how to buy a fund on a monthly plan, it's as easy as signing your name. All you have to do is fill out a preauthorized checking plan and a fund-purchase application. They're often on the same form. It won't take you more than a minute.

"Each month, the fund will forward you a summary of your current situation: how much you contributed this month; how many shares that money bought and at what price; your accumulated share position; everything. These statements explain it all. You just stick them in your file and watch the money grow, all the while thinking what a great guy your barber is.''

"Do they mail you the shares each month?''

"No. For convenience' sake, the shares are kept in non-certificate form at the mutual fund company. But if you ever want a share certificate, it's only a letter away."

"What if you want to cash out and get your money?"

"That's only a letter away, too. But you won't be doing that for a long, long time, will you, Tom?"

"Of course not, Roy. I was just curious."

I cut in, "What about taxes, Roy? Do you pay them each year?"

"You pay tax each year on any dividends that the mutual fund has declared. You see, mutual funds make money in three ways. Most of a growth fund's profit occurs when a fund sells stock for more than it paid for it—in other words, a capital gain. However, a fund also makes money when one of the stocks it owns pays the fund a dividend. Finally, a fund earns interest income from bonds and idle cash. At least once a year the fund declares dividends to distribute the profits from all three of these sources. By the way, it's very important that, at the time of purchase, you instruct the fund management to reinvest your dividends by purchasing additional shares of the fund. That's when the compounding effect really kicks in."

"That sound great, Roy, but if I'm reinvesting the dividends, where do I get the money to pay the tax owing?" I interjected worriedly.

"From your father," Roy deadpanned. "No, the dividend distributions are usually small and, therefore, so is the tax liability. It will not be enough in the early years to even discuss. In the later years you'll be so wealthy it won't be a problem then either." It was plain from Roy's tone he did not mean the last line sarcastically. "In addition to your very small annual tax on the declared dividend, obviously you must also pay tax on the capital gain when you sell some or all of your mutual fund shares. However, I hope by that time Congress has come to its senses and that the capital-gains tax has either been eliminated or reduced. We need to encourage, not discourage, investment. It's important to note that, on selling, you do not have to pay tax again on reinvested dividends—not even the IRS would try that.

"It's also important to note that if you've kept all your purchase statements, and I advise you to do so, and if you are selling some, but not all, of your accumulated shares, there is an excellent tax strategy available. Instruct the fund company to sell the shares for which you paid the most. By telling them the date of purchase of those shares and the price, they'll be able to honor your request. Moreover, it may not hurt to ask them for a written confirmation verifying that you sold the highest-cost shares in case Uncle Sam comes calling. By employing this strategy, you create smaller taxable profits and defer tax for a while—not eliminate, of course, but simply defer.

"One final point before we leave mutual funds. Another major reason mutual funds are preferable to just leaving your money in the bank is that they're somewhat less accessible. Very few of us have the willpower to resist the temptation that a growing bank account poses. As a result, a lot of people dip into their savings."

"You said mutual funds are probably our number one choice for investing the ten percent. What are the others?"

"Dave, my boy, there are literally hundreds of options. You could buy gold, Chinese ceramics, stamps, whatever. But for obvious reasons, those are not good choices. Certainly, mutual funds are almost perfect for our monthly savings—"

"That is, a well-selected mutual fund," I interrupted.

"That is, a well-selected mutual fund," Roy confirmed amiably. "But there is one other viable alternative. Surprisingly, it's the one Tom joked about earlier: real estate."

"How do you buy real estate for two hundred dollars a month?" Cathy and Tom chimed in stereo.

"Alas, with only two hundred a month it may be impossible, but with four or five hundred, it's very possible.

"Personal loan rates—car loans, for example—are running around twelve percent right now. If you borrowed eighteen thousand and amortized the loan, paid it back in full, in other words, over five years, it would cost you around four hundred dollars a month.

"But let's say instead of using the eighteen thousand to buy a car, you used it as a down payment on a seventy-two-thousand-dollar house. Your mortgage would obviously be for fifty-four thousand—somewhat less than five hundred dollars a month. You then rent the house out for that amount plus utilities and upkeep.

"The end result is that the rental income covers your mortgage. Your expenses are covered by your tenant. Your only cost is your monthly loan payment of four hundred bucks.

"Five years later, you sell the house for a hundred thousand dollars, a realistic figure representing an average annual compound return of less than seven percent. Your personal loan of eighteen thousand is no longer around . . . You've paid it off. The outstanding principal on your mortgage is around fifty-one thousand, as most of your monthly payment has been applied to the interest on the mortgage balance. One hundred minus fifty-one is forty-nine. You are left with forty-nine thousand dollars, less, of course, your tax liability on the capital gain."

"It's too easy," Tom snorted.

"Not only that," James Murray added, "but there can be some tax advantages to using borrowed money to buy real estate."

"Then why isn't every man, woman, and child doing it?" I asked.

"You'd be surprised how many people are doing it, or something similar to it. It's said that ninety percent of the world's millionaires have become millionaires through real estate. Mind you, it isn't as easy as it sounds. There are potential problems.

"The main one is, what happens if the property value declines instead of rising? People in New England who bought in the mid-eighties are still trying to recover. In many cases, their proceeds from a property sale wouldn't even cover the mortgage balance. They have negative savings! That's a frightening concept.

"With real estate, it's a matter of timing. There's no dollar cost averaging here. No safety net. So, you'd better be right when you buy that property. The one big thing investors do have in their favor, though, is real estate's relatively consistent record of rising prices. It seldom collapses. In fact, in some locales, it rarely falls at all, but . . . but . . . '' Roy wagged his finger.

"The only thing worse than a bad investment is a bad investment made with borrowed money. Dave, can you see yourself telling your wife that you just lost twenty thousand dollars, twenty thousand borrowed dollars?''

"She'd kill me,'' I gulped, knowing the prediction was accurate.

"Kill yourself first,'' Tom suggested helpfully.

"The timing of the purchase isn't the only problem. Interest rates can turn against you, too. Sure, they're reasonable now, but what if you have a variable-rate mortgage and interest rates hit eighteen percent? Then all of a sudden your mortgage payment skyrockets to around seven hundred and fifty dollars. The heartbreak of negative cash flow results. Say this happens at a time when your business is suffering, too, Cathy. What do you do?''

"Sell.''

"Sounds good, but with rates that high, very few people can afford to buy. Demand is way down, and a lot of people are trying to sell. You're not the only one hurt by the higher financing costs! End result: Your property value is down. If you have no choice but to sell, you'll have to sell at a loss,'' he ended ominously.

"Roy, you're scaring them off the finest investment a person could make!'' James Murray complained. "I mean, really, how many people do you know who have lost money in real estate?''

"I just want the kids to be aware there are risks.''

"That's fine, but—''

"Hold on, hold on. Let me finish. The other problem with real estate is that it has a very high PITA factor. Finding tenants, fixing toilets at two in the morning, mowing lawns . . . it's a lot of work. Some people thrive on that stuff. They're great with their hands and real estate provides them with a profitable way to enjoy their hobby. But if you're not that type of person, beware."

"The only thing I've fixed in my life is my cat," Tom kibitzed.

Jimmy and Clyde loved that one.

"So, I gather you're endorsing the fund route?" By now, my sister was on the edge of her seat.

"Initially, yes. In your early years of saving ten percent, I think the funds are a better way to go. You're busy starting your careers, raising families, buying homes, and all that. Real estate takes a lot of time. Also, the funds make more sense from a diversification standpoint, in that you'll probably own your own homes soon, so you'll already have some real estate.

"Besides, many people in their twenties, thirties, and early forties aren't in good enough financial shape to qualify for a down-payment loan, anyway—unless, of course, they borrow it privately or have a co-signer.

"What I did, and what I think you should do, is buy mutual funds with the ten percent for several years. When I had built up a good nest egg, I switched to real estate. Forgive the pun, but you don't want all your eggs in one basket. Plus, because I had a nest egg, I knew that if interest rates rose or real-estate prices dropped, I wouldn't be forced to sell. I had the luxury of being able to be patient. Patience is always one of the most valuable attributes in investing, and nowhere is that more true than in real estate. It may go down, but it seldom stays there.

"I've kept you three a long time today. Longer than I had planned." By the time Roy said this, Tom and I had long since had our haircuts finished. In fact, Tom needed a trim already. James Murray's gray hair was now joining our locks on the floor.

"I want to tell you a quick story before I let you go," Roy stated. "But before I do, are there any questions?"

"Should we buy more than one fund?"

"Well, Cathy, a fund, by its very nature, offers solid diversification, so I really don't think it's mandatory, although it probably wouldn't hurt. In fact, yeah, maybe using two or three funds would be a good idea."

"You talked a lot about selecting a mutual fund, but what about selecting a property?" I inquired.

"Talk to a professional. We're in the presence of greatness right here," he indicated, acknowledging James Murray. "In Ann Arbor, Dave, you'll have to locate someone with a good reputation. It shouldn't be hard. Ask around. In addition, there are a plethora of good real-estate books available at the library that talk about everything from selecting a good location to the tax implications of owning a property. No questions, Tom?"

"Just one. What's a 'plethora'?"

"I have another question," Cathy announced above the laughter. "What about IRAs and paying down debt? Aren't those supposed to be smart things to do? Wouldn't they be wise investments for the ten percent?"

"Those are excellent investments, and we'll talk about both of them in the upcoming months. But the ten percent saving is different. It's separate. It's our *I've-made-it-big* fund, and it's intended to give us the finer things in life. The things we dream of one day owning and couldn't afford otherwise—a luxury sedan, a winter home, early retirement . . . in Tom's case, a girlfriend.

"And the beauty of it is, it's not hard to do. The so-called sacrifice is barely noticeable. By saving ten percent of your pay now, you virtually guarantee yourself financial freedom later in life. Only a fool would say no to that. So, start now, and don't stop!"

"In the words of Syrus, 'Many receive advice; only the wise profit from it,'" James Murray elaborated. "Just thinking about saving ten percent has never made anyone wealthy."

"Like I said, I have just the story to convince you before you go," Roy remembered. "It will be of particular interest to you, Dave, because the individual involved is a teacher, too.

"Three or four years ago, a fellow came in. He explained that he wasn't here simply for a haircut, but also because he had heard that I'm a financial planning expert. 'I don't know a thing about insurance, stocks, real estate . . . any of that stuff,' he confessed. 'The only thing I know about financial planning is to save ten percent of all you make and invest it for long-term growth. The rest of it's Greek to me.'

"Well, it turns out this man's father had been a friend of Old Mr. White's and he, too, had been fortunate enough to have learned the golden secret. He passed it along to his young son but, unlike me, this teacher hadn't furthered his knowledge of financial planning. As he said, he knew nothing about insurance and investing. What's worse, I learned through our conversation that he had abused credit cards over the years, not started an IRA, and had lost all fifteen thousand dollars of an inheritance playing the commodities market."

"This is a real upbeat story, Roy. Very encouraging," Tom drawled, tongue in cheek.

"At the time of our meeting, that teacher's net worth was almost six hundred and fifty thousand dollars, Tom. Some of it, maybe one hundred and fifty thousand, represented his home and personal belongings. The rest of it had been created from his ten percent fund. What's more, his wife had chosen to work for only four years."

"He did everything else wrong but—" Cathy started.

"Because he had saved ten percent of each paycheck and invested it for long-term growth, today he's in great shape," Roy finished.

He then walked purposefully over to the counter. A second later, we heard two clicks. Roy then turned and handed my sister a cassette tape of our entire conversation.

"I thought this might come in handy for those who don't take shorthand," he commiserated, looking pointedly at me.

"Good," I laughed. "It will save Cathy having to transcribe her notes for us. Well, Roy, what does next month's 'adventure in accumulating' hold in store for us?"

"For now, why don't you three just worry about implementing this month's suggestions?" Roy responded.

"It's inspiring to know how wealthy Roy is," Tom cracked within earshot of Roy as we walked back out into the downpour. "But don't you think we're insulting him by offering to pay for our haircuts?"

"You boys," came Roy's rejoinder, "are all wet."

Chapter 5

Wills, Life Insurance, and Responsibility

"WELL, WELL," ROY GREETED US as we came in from the sunshine. "Has it been a month already? It seems as though you three were here just last week."

"They say time flies at your age, Roy," Tom laughed.

"Cathy, you look gorgeous, as always. Tom, you don't. Hey, Dave, when's school out? Your vacation must start soon."

"Week after next. Sue and I will stick around Ann Arbor until mid-July, and then we'll be here for five fun-filled weeks at the summer home we've rented in Lexington. You should drop by for a barbecue one night, Roy . . . but don't tell Clyde," I added loudly enough for Clyde to hear. He just smirked and doffed his Cleveland baseball cap.

"Roy, you're going to be really proud of us," Cathy began, always one to turn a conversation serious. "All three of us have started our save-ten-percent programs."

"That's great! Did you use preauthorized checking to buy mutual funds?" Roy asked.

"Cathy and I did," I answered. "Tom went another route. But before he tells you about it, I've got a quick story for you. I was passing on what you taught us to some

61

teachers in the staff room. They couldn't believe those compound interest examples. Even the math teachers were amazed! I explained why a monthly purchase plan of mutual funds was such a good idea: dollar cost averaging, forced savings, long-term growth . . . even the low PITA factor. Everything. Most of the teachers seemed really interested, but a couple were skeptical. Then Mary McGrath, an older English teacher, spoke up. She said that fifteen years ago, she had started a preauthorized checking plan to purchase a well-known growth fund, with one hundred dollars a month. She has had all her dividends reinvested and has never withdrawn a cent. Today, her fund is worth almost seventy thousand dollars . . . and that's with only one hundred a month over a mere fifteen years! I'll tell you, that impressed them! When one of the teachers in his mid-forties asked if it was too late for him, Mary replied, 'The best time to plant an oak tree was twenty years ago. The second best time is now.' Great line, huh?''

''I couldn't have said it better myself.'' Roy nodded approvingly. ''Obviously, starting young will benefit you tremendously, but so will starting today. Oh sure, you won't save as much starting later, but even a forty-five-year-old can still save a significant sum—very significant. As you pointed out, look what your teacher friend has accomplished in only fifteen years with a fairly small monthly saving.''

''I was in my mid-forties when I started paying myself first, and I've done real good,'' Clyde contributed.

''I've done really well,'' I corrected him.

''You too, Dave? That's great,'' was his quick comeback.

''So, Tom, what's this other route?'' Roy inquired slowly, probably still stunned by Clyde's unusual display of wit.

''Well, Roy, I know that you recommend mutual funds over real estate in the early years, but I had an opportunity I couldn't turn down.

"I told my brother what you taught us last month and he was really pumped up. He suggested that he and I go together to buy a property. The place next door to his had been for sale for a couple of months. It needs some work, but it has definite possibilities. Brian said that if we bought it together, he would do all the yard work, and all the repairs and renovations. My job would be to find a reliable tenant and handle the paperwork. We had James come out and take a look, and he agreed that, with the proximity to the water, the size of the lot, and the good neighborhood, the property was definitely underpriced. The deal closes next month.

"We're borrowing twenty-two thousand dollars against Brian's house and amortizing the loan over five years. That's going to cost us less than two hundred and fifty dollars a month, each. We're putting eighteen thousand dollars down and using the other four thousand to fix the place up a bit. Our mortgage is for forty-six thousand. Principal, interest, and taxes are going to cost us around five hundred and twenty dollars a month."

"Have you found a tenant?" Roy asked.

"That's the beautiful part, Roy," Tom answered eagerly. "Kyle MacKenzie and his wife have signed a three-year lease with us for five hundred and forty a month, plus utilities."

"It really is a sweet deal, Roy," James Murray broke in. "In five years I wouldn't be surprised if the place was worth a hundred thousand or more, especially after Brian's improvements. They've got a good tenant, balanced cash flow, low interest-rate exposure, and Tom All-Thumbs here doesn't even have to get his hands dirty."

"What's more, Roy, Brian assures me that if I were ever laid off he'd handle the loan payments until I got back on my feet—he's got the cash flow."

"I'm impressed, Tom. 'You done good,' as Clyde would say. I still think that, for most young people, mutual funds are the best alternative, but you're a good example of why the word 'always' is a dangerous one."

"Thanks, Roy. It's funny, but on the way here, all three of us agreed that, even though it's only been one month, we feel a lot better about our finances already. For the first time in my life, I actually believe I will be wealthy someday. It's great."

"Yeah, Roy, and you know what else?" Cathy beamed. "As Tom said, it's only been a month, but I haven't missed that ten percent at all, just as you promised."

"Don't get a big head, Roy. Your advice last month may have been great, but I'm not all that happy with my haircut," I kidded.

"I guess I'll have to get a new bowl," Roy quipped. "Are you three ready for the second lesson? I'd better warn you, it's not quite as exciting—"

"Or as long, I hope," Tom interjected.

"Or as long," Roy confirmed. "But, in a different way, today is just as important. We're going to look at estate planning. You know . . . wills, life insurance . . . those fun things."

"And to think that I looked forward to this for a month," Cathy groaned.

"Maybe wills and insurance aren't the most thrilling topics in the world, but they sure are important. And what's more, more people foul up in this area than any other part of financial planning.

"Way more than half the people I know don't even have a will. That's ridiculous. And as for life insurance . . . well, most Americans have the wrong kind, the wrong amount, and often even have the wrong person insured."

"Yeah. I read an article the other day saying that the majority of Americans are overinsured," I pointed out, thinking that for once I'd look informed.

"Wrong," Roy replied. "Dead wrong. Being one of the most insured countries on a per capita basis and being overinsured are not synonymous. Americans, for the most part, are not overinsured. Some obviously are, but the majority of us are underinsured—in some cases, dramatically, even alarmingly so.

"But we'll talk more about insurance in a few minutes. First I want to deal with wills.

"You know, estate planning is really nothing more than what you do before you die to make sure that the people and things that you care about are well taken care of after your death. You want your *living estate*, in other words, your assets less your liabilities, combined with your insurance proceeds, to provide the necessary capital to carry out your wishes. Your will should make sure that that capital is distributed according to your wishes.

"The importance of an up-to-date will cannot be overstated. Contrary to what most people believe, if you die without a will, things will not automatically work out as you would have wished. Disaster can result.

"Dave, let's say your father were to die tomorrow. If he didn't have a will, what do you think would happen?"

"My mother would inherit everything?" I hazarded, shrugging my shoulders.

"No. I bet the court decides. They'll look at how many children there are, how old they are, and all that stuff," Cathy ventured, in a somewhat more confident tone.

"You're both wrong," Roy stated. "When no will is available, the estate assets are frozen and the court winds up the deceased's affairs and pays off his or her debts. The remaining estate is then divided according to a rigid set of rules found in the state's intestacy laws."

"Intestacy?" Cathy and Tom echoed in chorus.

"Intestacy, from intestate: having made no will," Roy explained.

"No thought is given to the deceased's known wishes or to the needs of the potential inheritors. For example, even if a surviving spouse needed a great deal of money for medical reasons, the estate would still be allotted according to the rules. The bulk of the estate might be tied up in a trust for the children.

"In our state, and the rules do differ from state to state, if your father died intestate, the first sixty thousand dollars, along with some other allowances, would go to your mother. The remainder of the estate would be divided, one-half for your mother, one-half for you two kids."

"So, Mom would still get the lion's share," I summarized.

"Lion's share, yes, but I think you'll agree with me that it's your dad's wish for your mom to have everything and then, upon her death, for you children to inherit the family estate. Who knows? Over the years she may need the entire amount."

"Boy, you two had better hope your dad doesn't have a will," cracked Jimmy.

"Charitable donations, scholarship awards, gifts for grandchildren or godchildren . . . none of these will be taken care of if there is no will.

"Even if you're single, you should have a will. Cathy, if you died tomorrow, your entire estate would go to your parents. That may be what you want but, more than likely, it isn't," Roy continued.

"You're right, Roy, it isn't. I'd like to leave Dave and Sue something. I mean, they need it more than Mom and Dad do. And I'd like to leave the Big Sister organization something for all the fine work they do. And Dave and Sue have asked me to be godmother to their baby. I never thought about it before, but I really do need a will."

"Me, too," I added. "When I die, I want to make sure everything goes to Sue and doesn't get tied up in a trust for years. That's no good."

"Even I need a will," Tom mused. "I'm not really all that close to my dad, and even if I was, he certainly doesn't need the money as much as my older sister does. And I wouldn't mind leaving something to Brian either—at least my half of the house we're about to buy."

"Don't forget your best friend, either," I reminded him.

"All right. I don't think it's necessary to go around the room stating why each of us needs a will, or you'll end up being here longer than you were last month. The point is that everyone does need a will, period. We haven't even talked about problems that intestacy can cause for common-law spouses and business partners. It gets pretty scary."

"How do you make a will?" Cathy wondered.

"Don't do it yourself. I can't stress enough the importance of that bit of advice. Go to a professional. Many lawyers have experience in drawing up wills and in estate planning. They know the ins and outs of the various estate-planning alternatives, so seeking out their advice is *mandatory*. For instance, it is sometimes advisable to set up, in place of or in conjunction with a will, a *revocable living trust*. This particular type of trust allows you to retain control of your assets while at the same time letting you designate the assets to whomever you wish, whenever you wish, even prior to death, if you want to. Because of their flexibility, and because they allow your estate to bypass the often time-consuming and costly probate process, revocable living trusts in some cases are more efficient than wills. Note the phrase 'in some.' Living trusts are not for everyone. Because the initial setup costs are relatively high and there are ongoing maintenance and updating costs, living trusts are frequently best suited to larger and more complicated estates. Again, this underscores the importance of seeing a good lawyer. He or she can help you develop an estate plan that suits your specific situation. Everything from guardians for dependents to a *living will* should and will be covered."

"A living will—I've heard of that. It's a document that states that a terminally ill person doesn't have to be kept alive by artificial means," a once-again well-informed Cathy chipped in.

"Precisely," Roy concurred. "Often a very prudent thing to look into. Another wise move is to discuss with your lawyer the granting of power of attorney. Obviously, there is no way of predicting when you may become temporarily or permanently incapacitated. In the tragic event that that happened, a power-of-attorney agreement can be key to your family weathering the storm."

"Boy, I can see why using a lawyer's services is vital," I consented. "Is there anything we should do before consulting a lawyer?"

"Before you go to a lawyer, sit down and map out exactly what your estate would consist of and how you want it to be divided. If you're married, make sure your spouse sits down with you.

"Then choose an executor. This is the person or institution that will carry out your will's instructions. The executor may have to do everything from providing a complete inventory of your assets, to collecting money owed to you, to paying off your debts, to filing all proper tax documents, to distributing your estate, and more. It is a heavy responsibility.

"So, if you choose an individual as an executor, make sure he or she lives near you. It's unfair to ask your cousin Eddy to fly across the country to wind up your affairs, especially since it may involve several trips. Also, choose someone your age or younger. It doesn't make sense to name your father or aunt as executor, when the odds are they'll predecease you. And don't be too quick to name your spouse! If he or she has no money management skills, there may be other, more suitable choices. Besides, your spouse is going to have a hard enough time without having to handle all the work involved in being an executor. Co-executors are a good alternative. Your spouse and a friend with a business background, or your spouse and a financial institution with a reputable estate division, would both be perfect. Two final points about choosing an executor. One: For obvious reasons, choose someone who is absolutely honest and reliable. Two: Don't forget to name contingent executors in case your first choice is unwilling or unable to act when the time comes."

"Boy, you sure were right, Roy," Tom commented.

"About the importance of a will?"

"No. About this not being as exciting as last month."

"Ha, ha! Actually, you'll find the part on insurance very interesting. Just let me wrap up wills.

"Also, keep in mind that a change of state of residence, business ownership, divorces, alimony, remarriages, et cetera, et cetera, all can complicate the estate-planning process. Make sure the lawyer you're using is fully aware of any potential problem areas. Lawyers know how to plan for all the standard problems, like the simultaneous death of two spouses, but they're not mind readers. They can't know all the relevant details of your personal situation unless you tell them.

"A final point to keep in mind is that you must keep your will updated. Births, deaths, divorces, business deals, whatever, may make a will obsolete. Review your will at least once a year and, for heaven's sake, make sure that your executors know where to find it! In fact, give them a copy and keep another copy at your lawyer's.

"Oh, and always keep a complete, up-to-date net-worth statement, listing everything you own and everything you owe, along with a copy of your will, in your safety deposit box and at home. A friend of mine died ten years ago and they didn't discover until last year that he owned shares in a number of large companies. The certificates were registered in the brokerage company's name and held on account, and the firm had never been notified of his death. A lawyer I know tells me this kind of thing happens frequently."

"How much does it cost to draw up a will?" I inquired.

"A straightforward will, the kind most of us need, usually costs around two to three hundred dollars, sometimes less. In view of its importance, that's certainly not a lot of money to spend."

"I don't know why, but I always figured a will would cost a lot more than that."

"No. It's not the cost of a will that prevents most Americans from having one. It's just pure procrastination. We all know we're going to die someday, but we don't want to admit that day could be soon, so we put off planning

69

for it. But you three won't do that. Do you know how I can be so sure?''

''Because you know we're responsible people?'' Tom speculated.

''No. Because next month each of you is going to bring me a copy of your lawyer's bill showing that you've had a will drawn up. If you don't, the fountain of your financial knowledge will suddenly dry up.''

''Roy,'' Cathy protested, ''we're not little kids. We're mature adults.''

''Speak for yourself!'' Tom roared.

''We all started our save-ten-percent program without being forced to, didn't we?'' my sister persisted.

''Good point, Cathy. Very good point. But bring me the bill anyway,'' Roy commanded, over the chuckles of James Murray.

Procrastination is my middle name, but I didn't need Roy's strong-arm tactics to get me moving. After learning about intestacy laws, I decided that only a fool wouldn't have a will. A few hundred dollars is an insignificant price to pay when you consider what's at stake.

''The bottom line is, Roy, that if you don't have a will, your loved ones could suffer,'' I concluded aloud. ''I'm not going to do that to my survivors.''

''Well said, Dave. But bring me the bill next month anyway.''

''Roy did the same thing with me,'' Clyde piped up. ''Treated me just like a kid. You know what I did to get him back? I bequeathed him my little dog.''

''I can't believe that,'' James Murray scoffed.

''It's true. You can ask Roy.''

''No, no. Not the part about the dog. What I can't believe is you knowing the word 'bequeath'!''

''I hate to break up this scintillating dialogue, but we've got more material to cover.'' Roy's announcement immediately silenced Port Huron's Laurel and Hardy.

''On to insurance. Let me caution you now to pay strict attention to the rest of today's lesson. I say this for four reasons. One: The financial future of your loved ones may depend on you having the proper amount of life insurance. Two: It is, without a doubt, essential to your own financial future that you have the right type of life insurance. Three: There is a good chance that James and I are the only two people you'll ever meet who have a full understanding of insurance, and who are willing to share that understanding with you. And four: My tape recorder is broken."

"What about insurance agents?" Cathy asked.

"Are you kid—"

"Whoa, slow down, James. Slow down," interrupted Roy. "We'll talk more about insurance agents in a few minutes. For now, suffice it to say that there are some good insurance agents and some who are not so good."

"Many who are not so good," James Murray grumbled.

"Perhaps," Roy agreed. "But that holds true in any occupation. There are good teachers and bad teachers, good real-estate agents and bad real-estate agents—"

"And really bad real-estate agents," Clyde shot at James.

"The problem with insurance is that most people are so poorly informed that they have no way of telling the good agent from the bad agent. If I consistently give you a bad haircut, you'll eventually stop coming here."

"Gee, we haven't yet," I remarked.

"Cute, Dave. But with an insurance agent's advice, it's different. It's intangible. Its worth can only be measured by an informed observer. So, the answer is simple: Become an informed observer! Fortunately, that's not as difficult as you might think.

"Let's get started. Cathy, why do people buy life insurance?" Roy asked.

"Well, if you die prematurely, you want to have enough money to support your spouse and kids, I guess."

"Close. People buy, strike that, *should* buy life insurance so that when they die, their living estate, again, that is their assets less their liabilities, combined with their insurance proceeds, can allow for the proper winding down of their financial affairs, and provide the desired standard of living for their dependents. Now, that's pretty basic, isn't it?''

A collective ''yes'' was offered.

''Fine.'' Roy nodded as he turned back toward Cathy. ''Bearing that in mind, how much insurance do you need, Cathy?''

''I just bought a fifty-thousand-dollar policy.''

''I didn't ask how much you have. I asked how much you need,'' Roy reminded her politely.

''Apparently not fifty thousand dollars,'' Cathy frowned. ''I don't know . . . I guess . . . '' She paused to think.

''How much would your dependents need?'' Roy helped.

''I don't have any dependents,'' my puzzled sister responded.

Roy nodded his head slowly and emphatically.

''None. You're saying I don't need any life insurance?'' she asked.

''That's precisely what I'm saying. Life insurance is a wonderful thing. It is, no doubt, the most important of all financial products. It is a must until a sufficient living estate has been acquired to protect one's dependents. Purchased properly, it provides people with a relatively inexpensive way to guarantee their dependents a targeted standard of living if premature death occurs. Really, life insurance is better termed *financial protection for dependents*, or *income replacement insurance*. But despite all that, you have to remember it is still an expense. The life insurance companies aren't giving it away. So, like everything else that costs money, you only want to buy it when you have a need for it.

''Think about car insurance for a moment. It's a wonderful product, too. But no one in his right mind would buy it if he didn't own a car. Well, buying life insurance when you have no need for it is equally foolish.''

72

"Shouldn't I at least have enough insurance to cover my funeral expenses?" Cathy wondered.

"In addition to taking care of your dependents, your living estate and your insurance proceeds combined must also allow for the proper winding down of your financial affairs. That includes eliminating all debts, settling taxes, treating business partners and employees fairly, and paying funeral expenses. If your living estate is sufficient to do that, no insurance is needed. For most single people, that's the case," Roy replied.

"Hmm . . . " Cathy started slowly. "My assets would definitely cover my debts and my funeral costs, with money left over."

"Mine, too," Tom realized. "As of right now, I don't have any debts, and the twenty-five-thousand-dollar group insurance coverage I get as a benefit at work should cover my funeral."

"Twenty-five thousand! That's a heck of a funeral," Clyde whistled. "I'll look forward to it, Tom."

"Theoretically, this sounds fine, Roy, but I have a few questions," Cathy persisted. "When I bought my policy last week, the agent insisted it was the smart thing to do for a number of reasons. Some of those reasons still seem to make sense, even though I have no dependents. The first is that my policy is also acting as a savings vehicle for my retirement. The second is that insurance is cheaper to buy when you're young. The third is that I should buy insurance now, when I know I can get it. I can't be sure that in five years, when I may need it, I'll still qualify for it."

"Nonsense, nonsense, and nonsense," muttered James Murray, still glaring at Clyde over his coffee.

"Quite frankly, James is right," Roy conceded. "None of those reasons holds water. You'll see that as we continue our lesson. In fact, if you pay close attention, you'll be able to explain yourself why each of those reasons for buying is 'nonsense.'

"Right now, though, I want to concentrate on how to

analyze your insurance needs properly. Tom, how much insurance do I need?"

"Zero. Your living estate, as you put it, is sufficient to provide for your wife and kids. You are, after all, the wealthy barber," Tom answered confidently.

"By George, I think he's got it!" Roy turned to me. "Dave, how much insurance should you buy on your baby's life?"

"Zero. No one is dependent on the baby," I replied, with equal confidence.

"Very good," our instructor said approvingly. "Although we love them dearly, children are financial liabilities, not assets. You don't insure a liability! If you had an uncle move in with you, eat your food, drink your beer, and watch TV all day, would you insure him? Of course not! He's a liability. Although parents would cringe at that comparison, I hope you three get the point.

"You only buy insurance when there is a definite need to protect your dependents and to help in winding down your financial affairs. Single people, therefore, often don't need insurance. Young married couples, especially those with children, almost always need insurance. The question for them then becomes not 'Do we need it?' but 'How much do we need?'

"Often the answer to that is, 'More than you think.' Your living estate, not including your non-investment assets, plus your insurance proceeds must provide enough capital to accomplish a number of things. One: All debt *must* be paid off. The last thing the surviving spouse needs is to be saddled with debt. Two: Enough capital must be available to cover future lump-sum obligations. This is something that is often forgotten . . . your funeral expenses, for example. A better example, though, would be college expenses for the children. It costs quite a bit of money to send a child to college. Although the child should be responsible for a fair amount of the total cost, he or she may need help. That money to help has to come from somewhere. It should be taken into account when analyzing insurance needs. Three: There must be enough capital and other sources of income present to provide sufficient cash flow to support your dependents. If you feel that your family would need forty thousand dollars a year to live comfortably and their non-investment income after your death would be only ten thousand, your living estate and insurance proceeds would then have to provide a block of capital sufficient to bring in the other thirty thousand dollars annually. How much is that? Well, unfortunately, most people arrive at that answer by assuming they will always be able to earn a guaranteed ten percent on their money. That assumption leads them to believe they need a capital pool of three hundred thousand dollars."

"I don't see any problem with that logic," I confessed.

"The problem, since you must invest this money ultraconservatively for obvious reasons, is that you can't be sure you'll always be able to earn a ten percent rate of return. When it comes to loved ones, you're better to err on the conservative side. I would base my calculations on an eight percent assumed rate of return—certainly an achievable rate even with a relatively conservative investment approach. So, to generate thirty thousand dollars, I would need a three-hundred-and-seventy-five-thousand-dollar pool of capital.

"The last thing your living estate plus insurance proceeds must cover is often totally neglected by people: *inflation!* Inflation is a widow's or widower's number one enemy. For example, an insurance program is designed so that a widow is left with an annual income of thirty-five thousand dollars, the desired amount. The problem is that the entire thirty-five thousand is needed to support the family; none is saved for the future. Ten years later, that thirty-five thousand may be worth only twenty thousand in purchasing-power terms. A middle-aged, untrained woman is forced to go back to work and, even then, the family has trouble surviving. Unlikely? Hardly! That's exactly what happened to my wife's aunt . . . and to many, many other people. Inflation's eroding effect on purchasing power is as relentless as compound interest's growth effect on monthly savings. It must be taken into account. It sometimes means buying up to an additional one hundred thousand dollars of coverage. But so be it. It must be done.

"Dave, let's look at your case. Pretend that it's a year from now. You've bought your home, and you and Sue are proud parents. How much insurance do you need? And how much insurance should you buy on Sue's life?"

"With our down-payment fund gone toward the purchase of the house, we won't have any investment assets to speak of, so the insurance proceeds are going to have to cover all of Sue's and the baby's needs," I started.

"Good," Roy commended me. "Continue."

"First, we'll have to have a lump sum available to eliminate our debts. I should say debt. The only money that we'll owe will be our mortgage of, say, eighty thousand.

"Future lump-sum obligations. Hmm . . . Davey Junior's college education, the funeral expenses, and within a couple of years, a new car."

"Ten thousand should give you a good start on the education costs. There will be eighteen years to invest the money and make it grow," Roy explained.

"And ten thousand for burial costs and ten thousand for the car. So, future lump-sum obligations total thirty thousand," I tallied. "Then there's the need for a sufficient income. You know, I don't want Sue to feel she has to work outside the home . . . especially before the baby's in school. So, I think I'm going to assume her income after my death will be confined to the ten thousand dollars a year she makes freelancing as a travel writer. To live comfortably, she'll probably need around thirty thousand a year. With no debt and no rent to pay, that should be plenty."

"You know what I would do, Dave?" Cathy suggested. "If she could live comfortably on thirty thousand dollars, I would buy enough insurance to give her an income of thirty-three thousand. You know why? So she could continue the save-ten-percent program without cramping her lifestyle.''

"You know, you kids aren't nearly as slow as your father says you are," Roy joshed. "That's great thinking, Cathy. Dave, I'm sure you'd agree that Sue deserves not only to live comfortably, but also to have the finer things in life. Well, you've learned how she can!''

"Thirty-three thousand it is," I concurred. "To create an investment income of twenty-three thousand a year, assuming an eight percent interest rate, I would need how much, Roy?''

"Now, you've forgotten that Sue would receive a Social Security benefit of—I'm guessing a bit—say, just under ten thousand a year, until your child reaches at least the age of sixteen. That income certainly has to be factored in, too. Actually, your child would also receive a Social Security benefit, but knowing your wife, I'm going to assume that amount would be set aside for the child's future . . . perhaps a down-payment fund," Roy advised.

"I hadn't thought of that," I reluctantly admitted. "All right, then, I need only enough insurance to spin off an income of thirteen thousand a year. I realize that the Social Security benefit stops when my child gets older but I'm sure that, by then, Sue will be back at work anyway—''

"Or remarried . . . to me," Tom smirked.

"How much coverage would I need, Roy?" I pressed on, undaunted.

"One hundred and sixty-two thousand and five hundred dollars," James Murray intervened, proudly showing Clyde the calculator on his watch.

"As for inflation," I went on, "I really don't think I'd need that much. With Sue saving ten percent and with her certain to re-enter the travel agency business when the baby gets a little older, she should be fine." I looked around smugly.

"Excellent, Dave," Roy congratulated me. "The last bit on inflation was very well thought out. That's the type of analysis we all have to do on our insurance needs. It is imperative that we not buy too little insurance, but it is also important that we not buy too much. Did you total how much insurance you decided you needed? Two hundred and seventy-two thousand five hundred dollars' worth."

I was dumbfounded.

"He won't be able to afford his premiums, will he?" asked Tom, who, uncharacteristically, seemed genuinely concerned.

"I get forty-five thousand dollars' coverage free with my benefit package, but I'll still have to buy almost a quarter of a million worth. I'll need the insurance," I griped. "Paying the premiums is going to kill me!"

"Dave, my boy, you're wrong. If you buy the proper types of insurance, your premiums will be quite reasonable. For now, though, let's stick to the amounts and not get ahead of ourselves.

"Making the same assumptions . . . house, baby, et cetera . . . how much insurance should you place on Sue's life?" Roy then asked.

"Sue's no longer working at the travel agency, so our current family income would only drop by the ten thousand dollars she makes selling her travel articles. But the expenses would also drop with one less person to support. With my income being fairly good, I'm going to say zero. No insurance on Sue's life."

"I can see your logic, Dave—" Roy conceded.

"But—" I anticipated.

"But I want to make two points. Always insure both spouses for at least the amount of the outstanding debt, in your case, eighty thousand dollars. A debt-free balance sheet substantially reduces stress, along with freeing up cash flow. Raising a child, making payments on an eighty-thousand-dollar mortgage, and enjoying a good standard of living wouldn't be easy on your salary alone. Also, you've forgotten a couple of expenses that would result from Sue's death. One: funeral costs of ten thousand dollars. Two: day care for your young child. With no debt, I'll agree that you won't need to replace the entire income from Sue's writing, but you want at least enough to cover the cost of child care."

"So, I probably need two hundred thousand dollars' coverage on Sue," I surmised. "Eighty thousand to pay off the mortgage, ten thousand for the funeral, and the rest to pay for a nanny for a few years."

"Again, don't forget to include any potential Social Security benefits in your analysis," James Murray reminded me.

"The point of all this was not just to help Dave." Roy motioned toward Tom and Cathy. "It's to help you two bored-looking individuals, as well. There may be a woman out there crazy enough to want Tom as a husband. There might be an even crazier man who would tolerate Dave as a brother-in-law. So, eventually you may both be in the position of needing insurance. And when you are, you've got to be able to figure out exactly how much you need. All it takes is the knowledge I've given you—remembering the four needs for insurance proceeds—and some common sense."

"I'm going to talk to my brother about this tomorrow, Roy." Tom shook his head disbelievingly. "He's got two young children and a wife. I now know for a fact that he doesn't have nearly enough insurance. He has one hundred thousand dollars' coverage through work, but that's it."

"You may be doing him the biggest favor of his life . . . or at least doing his loved ones the biggest favor of *his* life," Roy replied. "Now, before we move on to the different types of insurance, let me give you three illustrations of some tricky evaluations you may be faced with in the future.

"One: Both spouses are working and making excellent money. That situation could arise, for example, if Cathy married a doctor. They analyze their insurance needs and decide that if either of them died, the other could carry

79

on quite comfortably, at least financially, on his or her own without insurance proceeds. Their house is fully paid for, and their two children could easily be supported on either parent's income. What's wrong with their analysis?''

For a few seconds, everyone was silent. Then I realized where Roy was headed. ''What if they both die at the same time? Their children would be left with only the house.''

''Excellent, Dave! Does everyone see? James, didn't you tell me about a case just like that?''

''Yes. That happened to friends of Barb's parents several years ago. You have to protect against situations like that by buying a policy that pays only when both of the insureds die,'' James answered.

''All right. A second example,'' Roy continued without missing a beat as Tom got into the barber chair. ''Cathy sells half of her business to Joe Schmoe. A year later, Joe dies, leaving his half to his wife, who has no business experience. She has no desire to enter the business world and decides that she wants to sell her half back to Cathy. Unfortunately, Cathy has no liquid reserves and has exhausted her lines of credit. Suddenly her lifeline, Richardson Landscaping, is in jeopardy. Will it be shut down? Will Schmoe's half be sold to an inappropriate person?''

''I should have had insurance on *his* life. Is that what you're saying?'' asked Cathy.

''Yes. It's another example of how difficult it can be to analyze how much insurance to buy. It's not enough that you are properly insured so that your loved ones will be taken care of. You also have to make sure that anyone you're dependent upon is properly insured.''

Since I'm not dependent on anyone, this point didn't strike me as too important. It sure had an impact on Tom, though.

''Hey!'' he blurted out, stopping Roy in mid-snip. ''Lucky you gave that example! If my brother were to die after we close our real-estate deal, I'd be in trouble. I couldn't afford to pick up the payments on his half of the down-payment loan. I'm going to have to talk to him about us getting insurance on each other's lives.''

''Take care of that soon,'' Roy encouraged him. ''One final example of insurance-needs analysis. Thirty years from now, Tom has parlayed his monthly savings and apparent knack for buying undervalued properties into a three-million-dollar real-estate empire. Unfortunately, he is hit by a bus.'' This drew applause from both Jimmy and Clyde. ''A substantial estate tax is levied. Tom felt that he was self-insured, so the estate was limited to his personal residence, real-estate holdings, and baseball-card collection. So, his executor, Cathy, who, incidentally, was driving the bus''—this remark caused me to cough my Pepsi out onto my white golf shorts—''is forced to sell several properties to pay the tax bill. Sadly, real estate is at its lowest point in two decades, making it a terrible time to sell. But she has no choice. The point is that, for liquidity reasons, it would have been a good idea for Tom to carry enough insurance to cover his tax liability.

''I gave these three examples to show you that a lot of thought is needed to correctly analyze your insurance needs. Don't be lazy. Do the necessary thinking. Get a book out of the library. Talk to an insurance agent. They've had years of experience and have encountered almost every possible scenario. For heaven's sake, be insured for the correct amount! You owe it to yourself and to your family.''

It was now evident to everyone that Roy's promise of this month's lesson being shorter than last month's had a better-than-even chance of being broken. We hadn't even delved into the different types of insurance policies. I had nightmarish visions of Tom and me missing our tee-off time.

''Roy, I don't mean to sound unappreciative, because I'm far from it. I can't believe how much we've learned again today, but Tom and I are supposed to meet Dad at Black River in less than an hour. With all the different types of policies still to be discussed, could we perhaps finish this off next month?''

"That won't be necessary, Dave. Although, as you pointed out, there are a number of different types of policies, there is only one that you, Cathy, and Tom will probably ever need: *renewable and convertible term insurance*. It won't take me long to teach you why.

"I'm sure that even you three, with your limited financial backgrounds, have heard of the age-old argument of whole life versus term, better stated as cash-value insurance versus term insurance."

"I certainly have," Cathy remarked. "You won't believe this, but when I went to buy insurance last month, I actually decided to do a little research beforehand. All three books I read suggested that term insurance was a better alternative than cash-value insurance. Yet both agents I saw were very insistent that I buy cash-value. I bowed to their expertise."

"I don't even know the difference," Tom admitted candidly.

James Murray leapt in, "Those agents recommended cash-value because—"

"Hold on, James," Roy ordered. "You'll have your chance. First, let's look at a couple of definitions.

"Term insurance is like fire insurance. It pays out the face amount of the policy if the insured dies, just as fire insurance pays out the face amount if the insured building burns down. Term insurance is in force for a stipulated length of time, or term; hence its name. It's most often sold in one-year, five-year, ten-year, or twenty-year terms. When the term expires, so does the insurance. There are no cash values, savings, or investment elements. It is insurance in its most basic and least expensive form.

"Cash-value insurance is basically a combination of term insurance and a forced-saving program, with the savings program being the cash-surrender value of the policy. Or, in other words, the amount that you've built up in savings and that you would receive if you were to cancel the

policy. Dave, are the odds of you dying next year if
you own a cash-value insurance policy higher or lower
than the odds of you dying next year if you own a term
policy?''

"The same, of course. Even I know that."

"Yes, I think anyone could answer that question correctly. It's the significance of the answer that most people
miss," Roy explained patiently.

Damn. He had lost me. "I'm not sure I follow you."

"I'm sure you've heard the expression, 'Buy term and
invest the difference.' What does it mean to you?" Roy put
the ball back in my court.

"Well, instead of buying a cash-value policy, you buy
the same amount of term coverage, which is less expensive because it doesn't include a savings element. Then
you invest the difference between the two costs in a savings vehicle."

"That's right. So, remembering your answer to the
'odds of dying' question, what's wrong with the oft-heard
question, 'Am I better to buy term and invest the difference, or to buy a cash-value policy?' I'll tell you what's
wrong. They are the same thing. As you said, the odds of
dying are the same, regardless of what type of policy you
buy. So, there is really only one type of life insurance, and
that is pure protection based on a mortality table. That's
what term insurance is. Cash-value insurance is pure protection, or term insurance, plus a savings element. 'Buy
term and invest the difference' is exactly what a cash-
value policy does. The problem is, it doesn't invest that
difference nearly as well as you can on your own."

"If that's the case, why do insurance companies issue
cash-value products? And why do agents sell them?" asked
Cathy.

"Because both companies and agents often put their
own interests ahead of their clients'," James Murray
responded hotly, before Roy had a chance to speak. "The
premiums on cash-value policies are much higher—and so
is the commission rate! The companies and agents make

far more money by selling cash-value insurance than they could by selling term."

"You're pretty agitated, James!" Cathy exclaimed. "Do you agree with him, Roy?"

"No. With all due respect, James, I don't. Sure, there are a number of unscrupulous salespeople, but, as I said earlier, I don't think it's any worse in the insurance industry than in any other business. Maybe it was fifteen years ago, when James was an agent. But now many agents do a conscientious job not only of placing insurance, but also of estate and financial planning. The products have improved, and so have their prices. Now you can get price distinctions based on sex and based on smoking versus non-smoking, for example. Professionalism is definitely on the rise, too. More and more agents are becoming better educated about all financial matters, not just insurance."

"If all that's true, why do they sell so much of what you claim is an inferior product?" Cathy persisted.

"Yes! If all that's true, why do they sell so much of what you claim is an inferior product?" James Murray echoed.

"The policy I just bought on my agent's recommendation was a cash-value policy," Cathy remarked, before Roy could offer a response.

"First, let me say that not all agents do push cash-value policies. Many have seen the light and now sell primarily renewable and convertible term insurance. Many are also espousing the benefits of paying yourself first, saving ten percent, and building up an IRA or other retirement plan. Those people are doing good jobs for their clients.

"Second, those who do sell cash-value insurance believe they are doing the right thing. They believe, and rightly so, that it is vital not only to have the proper amount of coverage, but also to become self-insured through saving and investing. For obvious reasons, insurance costs increase dramatically later in life. So, you have to have saved the funds necessary to pay them, or to have saved enough not to even need insurance in your later years. Most agents feel a cash-value policy accomplishes this goal of saving while, at the same time, insuring you.

"They argue that although 'Buy term and invest the difference' sounds good in theory, it seldom works in practice. Why? Because for most people the more accurate expression is 'Buy term and spend the difference.' Agents see that a lot of clients don't have the discipline or the knowledge to invest the difference. So, even though they start out properly insured with inexpensive term coverage, they end up facing a retirement that includes high insurance costs and an empty bank account."

"Do most people end up that way?" I wondered.

"Unfortunately, a lot do. It's staggering the number of people over the age of fifty-five who are in serious financial trouble. But you won't be," Roy assured us.

"How can you be so certain?"

"Because you're getting financial advice from the wealthy barber. Between your ten percent fund and your retirement planning, you'll be self-insured at a very reasonable age—very reasonable. You're not only buying term and investing the difference; you're investing more. And you're investing it well!"

"That sounds great, Roy. But if the insurance company is offering to do it all for you by selling cash-value insurance—insurance plus savings—why not let them? Won't they do a better job investing than we would, anyway?"

Cathy's question seemed justified.

"No!" was Roy's resounding answer. "Normally, the savings portions of cash-value policies are comparatively poor investments! Tom, if I came to you and said the following, would you save with me? 'To save at our institution, you must buy life insurance. You must pay for it even if you don't need it. We'll take everything you deposit in the first year for ourselves. In future years, we'll charge you to deposit money into your savings account. You can borrow the money at any time, but we'll charge you interest. If you happen to die while this loan is outstanding, we'll decrease the amount we were to pay your beneficiary by the outstanding amount of the loan. If you don't borrow from this account and you die, we'll pay the beneficiary only the face amount of the policy—we'll keep your savings for ourselves. Oh, and finally, we don't offer the greatest rates of return.'"

"No, thanks. I think I'll keep buying houses with my brother. You know, I always thought it was too good to be true that you could often borrow from your insurance policy at a low interest rate. But paying any interest to borrow your own money isn't that good a deal, is it?"

"Say, Tommy boy. If you thought being able to borrow your own money from your policy at five percent was a good deal, you'll love my offer," James Murray wheedled facetiously. "I'll lend you your money out of your bank account and only charge you four percent! Sounds good, doesn't it?"

"You see," Roy went on, "the deal I offered Tom isn't far removed from the deal offered by the traditional cash-value policy. In a way, you can't blame insurance companies for trying to make money. They have to cover expenses, pay their agents, and make a profit for their shareholders. That can't leave much for you, the policyholder. To save successfully, you have to cut out the middleman—"

"And you have to invest for growth," a fervent Tom interrupted.

"A good point indeed. As we saw last month, the last thing we want is our long-term savings tied up earning low rates of return. We want to be owners, not loaners," Roy reminded us.

"You mentioned that if we buy a traditional cash-value policy and die, all we get back is the face value of the insurance we have paid for. The insurance company keeps our savings. That seems almost illegal," I remarked.

"That's one point on which James and I are in full agreement," Roy sighed. "For years, the insurance companies virtually stole the savings of many of their policy-holders. In fact, some companies still issue policies that keep the savings portion upon the death of the insured. That's not fair, and there is no defense for it, especially since most policyholders don't realize that the cash value belongs to the insurance company and not to them. Fortunately, many agents and companies are getting away from that type of product.''

"The premium you pay for those policies covers the costs of two services: protection for your dependents if you should die; and protection for yourself if you should live. You pay dearly for both those services but, unless you have mastered the impossible trick of being simultaneously alive and dead, you are restricted to receiving the benefits of only one service. It's a terrible deal!'' James Murray pointed out.

"There is one other point I'd like to make here. Some agents agree that cash-value policies might not be the best way to save, but argue that they're still worthwhile because they are compulsory savings plans. That,'' Roy snorted, "is nonsense. If you have the self-discipline to make premium payments over a long period of time, you certainly have the self-discipline to manage a suitable savings program on your own. In fact, you three have already started.''

"I'm confused by one thing.'' Cathy stared at Roy intently. "The cash-value policy I bought last week was a lot different than the traditional one you two are describing. It's called *universal life*, and my agent assures me that the rates of return are very competitive. He also told me that, when I die, my beneficiary gets both the insurance proceeds and the policy's savings component. In fact, I can even invest the savings in a vehicle similar to a mutual fund if I want to. That doesn't sound like a bad deal, does it?''

"Universal life is a great example of what I said earlier. The insurance industry really has improved its product line over the last few years. Universal life is a much better product than the traditional whole life policy. Most universal life policies unbundle the insurance and savings elements, meaning that when you die, as you said, your beneficiary will receive both. They also offer more competitive rates of return. That being said, though, for a couple of reasons universal life usually still isn't as good as buying term and investing the difference. First, the term insurance component may be purchased much more cheaply outside the package. Second, because the company has to cover expenses and make a profit, the investment-savings portion may not yield as great a return inside the package as outside. This is especially true if you cash in the policy in the early years, as the insurance company's fixed costs on each policy are very high. If, for example, after ten years you cancel your universal life policy because you no longer need the insurance, the rate of return on your savings component is often only in the three percent area—which is ridiculous. Third, you must buy your investment component from the same insurance company that you're buying your life insurance from, obviously, as they're two parts of a single product. This, equally obviously, may not be ideal.

"Universal life does have one major benefit, and that is that, at the moment, the savings portion is allowed to grow tax-free until withdrawal. But because of the sometimes inferior rates of return, the absence of reasonable long-term guarantees on both the investment and insurance sides, and the comparatively high costs of the term component, that advantage is usually negated. The bottom line still is—buy term and invest the difference. However, it can't hurt to talk with an agent and examine all your alternatives.

"Cash-value policies carry level premiums whereas term becomes more expensive as you get older. Why is that?" Roy tested us.

"I know," Tom stated. "It's because, with cash-value policies, you overpay in the early years to subsidize the rising costs in the later years. The overpayment is invested and compounded so the rising costs in later years are easily covered.''

"Tom, I'm impressed." Roy's compliment was genuine. "Is this a good thing?"

Tom spoke up again. "No. It's 'nonsense,' as James would say. Why overpay in the early years when there's a good chance you won't even need the coverage in the later years? I'll be self-insured by the time my term insurance costs become expensive. Also, when you're younger you need the money more. You have more responsibilities. It's a bad time to be overpaying for insurance.''

"Tom, I take back all the things I've thought about you over the years. You are definitely smarter than the average bear," remarked Roy.

"Bear, perhaps, but not human," I muttered, belying the fact that I was impressed.

"OK. I see that term insurance is the way to go, but what about my agent's argument that buying insurance now was a good idea so I would guarantee future insurability?'' Cathy absentmindedly pushed a fallen lock of hair with her toe. "That seems to make sense, doesn't it? Why did James label that as 'nonsense' ?''

"I'll answer that, Roy," James Murray offered. " 'Nonsense' might not have been the right word. Maybe it's a little strong. But I still don't think you should buy life insurance unless you need it. I believe only two percent of people are turned down for life insurance. Yes, there is a chance you might become one of them, but there's also a chance you'll be in a car accident today. I'm sure you'll still drive. In life, you can't avoid all risks. If you do insist on buying to guarantee insurability, though, make sure you buy term insurance so that, for the same premium dollars, you can guarantee as much insurability as possible.''

"Very diplomatically spoken, James. I'll hurry along so you two can make your golf game.''

"Yeah. If we miss that tee-off time, you'll wish you had insurance," Tom advised Roy with a wink.

"I mentioned the terms *renewable* and *convertible* earlier. Renewable means that, at the expiration of the stated term, you can renew the insurance without having to prove insurability by taking a physical. It's obvious why that's important. If you got cancer but weren't going to die before your term insurance expired, guaranteed renewability would be your salvation.

"It's often a wise move when you purchase renewable term insurance to ensure that your policy sets out the maximum rate that you can be charged on each of your future renewal dates. Why? To prevent the issuing company from allowing you to renew only at uncompetitive rates. Whether those uncompetitive rates arise through company design or are caused by some other phenomenon —AIDS, for example—you won't be protected unless your policy has guaranteed future premium costs.

"Usually, you're allowed to renew until age sixty-five or seventy. This will be more than sufficient for you three, because you'll all be self-insured long before then.

"Convertible means that the policyholder has the right to convert the face amount of the policy to any cash-value plan sold by the issuing company, again without proving insurability. This feature is important in case you need insurance past age sixty-five and can no longer renew your term insurance. I doubt if any of you will have to call on this feature, but buy it just the same. It's very cheap," Roy finished.

"I feel very strongly that no company should be allowed to sell non-renewable or non-convertible term insurance. The reasons are self-evident," remarked James Murray. "There are just too many ways the policyholder can get hurt."

"Also, when you buy your policy, buy *non-participating* insurance. Participating policies work like this: The issuing company adds a surcharge to your premium. Out of this surcharge, they pay you *dividends*. These are not dividends in the normal sense of the word—a partial distribution of after-tax profits. Instead, they are just rebates of surcharges. By law, the insurance companies cannot guarantee the amounts of the future dividend payments. Those amounts will be determined by the actuarial success of the company. Really, a participating policy is nothing more than a way in which the insurance company gets you, as a policyholder, to share the risk. No one should buy insurance to share risk. We buy it to attempt to eliminate risk. Don't buy a participating policy! Yes, occasionally a participating policy, thanks to the issuing company's strong actuarial performance, may end up being less expensive than a non-participating policy, but why chance it? There are better things to do with your money," Roy emphasized.

"Should we shop the market for the lowest rate?" was Cathy's next question.

"Yes," James Murray replied.

"No," Roy countered. "You should always attempt to get a competitive rate, but not necessarily the lowest rate. Many agents are restricted to offering only the products of the company they're licensed with. If you are dealing with such an agent, and he or she is doing a good job helping you to analyze your insurance needs and giving you other financial planning advice, it is probably prudent to stick with that agent. This may mean not getting the lowest rate. Your rate, however, should still be a competitive one. Too much loyalty can be expensive! It's also imperative that you pay attention to the quality of the insurance policy, not just its price. In layman's terms what I mean is this: You want to be sure that when or if the insurance company has to honor your family's claim it has the financial ability to do so. That should be obvious, yet many consumers pay no attention to the financial health of their insurance company. Yes, that responsibility should be partially borne by a good agent, but consulting A.M. Best and Company's ratings of the various insurance companies' financial strengths sure can't hurt.

"It's important to note that you probably won't be buying all your term insurance from an agent. A non-agent source of term insurance is the group insurance offered through work. Cathy, this won't apply to you at this point. Group insurance can, and I stress 'can,' be a great deal. Because it is distributed to the consumer more efficiently, group insurance is often an inexpensive alternative to an individual policy.

"There are some caveats with group insurance, though. It isn't always better than an individual policy. Group rates are based on the average person within the group. If you are substantially younger than your colleagues, you may be better off with an individual policy. Likewise, if you are female and the group policy has no distinction based on sex. Or if you are a non-smoker and the group policy has no distinction based on smoking. Get your group-rate quote from your company's personnel department and then get a quote from your agent for the costs of an individual policy. Also, if you leave your company, you may not be able to take your insurance with you on a convertible and renewable basis. That's not a good situation. Instead, almost all group policies allow you to convert to a cash-value plan within thirty-one days of leaving the group. We don't want cash-value, so only accept this conversion if you are unable to qualify for individual term insurance at the time of your departure. The fact that you don't have full control over your group coverage is not ideal. Depending on your individual situation, it may or may not be a problem. Make sure that you show your group policy to your life insurance agent. He or she will help you to evaluate its merits and drawbacks.

"Also, don't restrict your analysis of group policies to the one offered at your place of work. You may be able to qualify for a plan available through your university alumni, a fraternal society, or a union. Some of these plans are excellent."

"Tom's a card-carrying member of the Archie Fan Club. Do they have a group policy?" Cathy teased.

"I'm getting forty-five-thousand-dollars' coverage free at work. Should I take it?" I asked.

"Two months and that's our first stupid question. Not bad. Not bad. Take anything you can get for free, Dave," Roy replied, shaking his head.

"How much does term insurance cost?" I asked, hoping not to embarrass myself again.

"Let's look at your example, Dave. We decided that next year you'll need around two hundred and seventy thousand dollars coverage, and Sue will need around two hundred thousand. Well, using the forty-five thousand you get as a benefit and properly selected term insurance, perhaps purchased through group coverage at work—I'm speculating a bit, but you're probably looking at about forty dollars a month."

"That's it?" I was amazed. "I thought it would be hundreds a month."

"No. Term insurance is a bargain, no doubt about it. And the nice thing is that, as you get older and your cost per thousand dollars of coverage goes up, you'll have less need for insurance," Roy explained. "Your living estate will be increasing each year."

"What about disability insurance, Roy? Do I need it?"

"We'll talk about disability insurance and medical insurance in an upcoming lesson, Cathy."

"Next month?"

"No. Next month we're going to look at various retirement plans—IRAs, Keogh plans, pensions, et cetera."

"Should we bring our sleeping bags next month, Roy? It's almost Sunday, isn't it?" Tom kidded, as we headed for the door.

"All I'm doing for you three and that's how you treat me . . . Oh, the disrespectful youth of today. Hey, you two should score a little better this time out."

"Why's that?"

"It's after eleven o'clock. You're going to miss the first three holes."

"Ooh, wealthy and witty. What a deadly combination," I said with a grin, as we stepped back out into the sunlight.

"Don't worry about it." Tom patted me on the shoulder. "By the time we get to the course, your dad will have paid for our greens fees. Now, that's sound financial planning!"

Chapter 6

Planning for Retirement

"GOOD MORNING, DEAR FRIENDS," ROY greeted us enthusiastically. "What a fabulous day!"

"Actually, it's overcast and cool," I noted, looking to Tom and Cathy for verification.

"I'm talking about the positively glowing feeling permeating every fiber of one's being the day after a Tiger ninth-inning comeback victory," Roy beamed.

"You're making me sick," came from the recesses of the back room, where Clyde was stewing, and brewing coffee.

"How right you are, Roy." I smiled. "On days like this, it's just great to be alive."

"We're going down to tomorrow's game," Cathy informed him cheerfully. "Sue and Dave, and Tom and I. Oh, let me rephrase that. I'm going with Sue and Dave, and Tom is also coming."

"And to think I was going to pay for your ticket," sighed Tom, shaking his head.

"On a more serious note, does each of you have a photocopied bill to show me?" checked Roy, referring to last month's ultimatum to *get a will or else.*

Cathy had the honor of handing him all three documents.

"I'm impressed," he praised us. "You three really seem determined to get your financial affairs in order. I commend you."

"Not that we have much choice," I muttered.

"As I pointed out last month, when it comes to proper estate distribution, the importance of a will cannot be overstated. Where there's a will, there's a way."

Groan.

"You've been dying to use that line, haven't you, Roy—no pun intended," Tom added. "I'll bet you meant to use it last month, forgot, and spent the last four weeks in a state of depression. Right?"

"Of course not, Tom. It was a spontaneous, off-the-cuff remark," answered Roy, with a wink at James Murray.

"Before we get started with this month's lesson, I want to tell all of you that I canceled my life insurance policy," Cathy announced proudly. "Mind you, right after I told my agent, I regretted my decision."

"Why?" James Murray asked curiously.

"Because I thought he was going to kill me," Cathy chuckled.

"Yeah. Some salespeople don't handle rejection well. Did he ask you why you had changed your mind?"

"Yes, and when I explained all the reasons, he became quite indignant and said, 'A little knowledge is a dangerous thing.'"

"To which you replied?" I prompted her.

"To which I replied, 'You're right, so why don't you take some courses?'"

"That conduct is not indicative of most insurance agents' attitudes," Roy commented amid the laughter. "As I said last month, for the most part, they're a very professional group. That particular agent was probably upset because he mistakenly believed that he was acting in your best interest, and he was frustrated when you dismissed his advice."

"Bull," James Murray snorted. "He was annoyed that he had lost a commission."

"That too," Roy conceded. "Whatever his reason, his behavior was out of line and, as I said, not representative of insurance agents' behavior in general. Anyway, you did the right thing, Cathy. You have to do what's best for you, not what's best for the agent. If that means canceling or replacing a policy, so be it."

"If you want to replace an insurance policy because you've found a less expensive alternative, or because you're making the often intelligent move from a cash-value policy to a term policy, there is an important caveat to keep in mind. You shouldn't cancel the old policy until you have purchased the new one, just in case you're no longer insurable," James Murray explained from behind the sports section of the *Detroit News.*

"Good point, James!" Tom exclaimed. "I'll have to mention that to my brother. He and Carol are going to switch her policy to renewable and convertible term and do their saving on their own."

"Speaking of Brian, how's the real-estate deal coming along? Have you closed yet?"

"Yeah. We closed two weeks ago. We hadn't budgeted very well for some of the closing costs. Actually, we hadn't budgeted for them at all," Tom confessed. "Appraisal fees, title search, legal costs . . . all that stuff adds up! But everything worked out fine in the end, and Kyle and Cindy moved in last Saturday. The three of us couldn't believe all the little improvements my brother had made to the place. He'd spent less than a thousand dollars, but the house looked ten thousand dollars' worth better. Things like a bit of new trim make all the difference in the world. The guy is amazing."

"Sounds great, Tom," Roy responded. "It really is incredible what a handyman—"

"Handyperson," Cathy corrected.

"Handyperson," Roy acknowledged, "can accomplish with relatively little money. It looks as though Brian is the ideal partner. Did you two discuss your insurance needs?''

''We each bought a renewable term insurance policy, naming the other as beneficiary, with a face value of twenty-two thousand dollars that declines over the term of the loan—decreasing term insurance, the agent called it. If either of us dies, the survivor will be able to pay off our entire down-payment loan. Now it won't cause me any financial hardship if Brian happens to die. In fact, I'm encouraging him to take up hang gliding,'' Tom joked.

''Good thinking, Tom. Not the hang-gliding part, but the insurance. You're a surprisingly quick study,'' Roy reflected.

''What do you mean 'surprisingly'?'' Tom sputtered.

''Today, we're going to look at the various ways to save for your retirement,'' Roy continued, rendering Tom's question rhetorical. ''I'm sure everyone here would agree that it's imperative that all of us plan for the future—after all, we are going to spend the rest of our lives there!

''Recognizing that, I'm sure everyone here would also agree that it makes sense to develop a *retirement plan*— retirement being an important and lengthy part of that future. Basically, what we need to do is prepare a plan that will lead to prosperous 'golden years' without demanding too great a sacrifice today. That, in essence, is what good retirement planning is all about.''

''Building for the future without killing the present,'' Tom paraphrased—accurately, judging by Roy's nod.

''Today, we're going to look at a number of investment vehicles that will help you save for retirement, and we're going to learn to select those that are best suited to your needs within the boundaries of Tom's retirement-planning rule.

''It's crucial that you three pay close attention today. Statistics show that millions of Americans retire near— or under—the poverty level. In fact, it's believed that well over fifty percent of retired Americans need some form of government assistance to survive. That a situation like this exists in a country that has enjoyed our level of economic prosperity is nothing short of embarrassing. Nowhere is the average person's lack of financial acumen more glaringly evident."

"We won't need government assistance," Cathy piped up. "Our ten percent fund will take care of any income problems. Don't forget that in May you guaranteed us that someday we'd be wealthy."

"Yeah, and not only will we have our ten percent funds, we'll also be drawing Social Security payments! This retirement planning thing isn't going to be painful at all. We just have to continue doing what we're doing now," Tom added hopefully, no doubt knowing in his heart that this argument wasn't going to wash with Roy.

"Not so fast," our mentor interjected, to no one's surprise. "You have brought up a good point, but your conclusion is faulty.

"I'll back my guarantee of your future wealth one hundred percent. But the ten percent fund is not intended to augment our retirement income. It's our I've-made-it-big money. It's our I-can-now-do-and-buy-anything-I-want capital. A mansion on the lake, a condominium in Fort Lauderdale, a fancy car . . . these are the reasons we're saving ten percent of our net income," Roy concluded emphatically.

"But by that time we'll have so much that if we happen to be a bit short on the income side, we can just tap into our ten percent fund, can't we?" Cathy asked meekly.

"Ah, but we'd prefer not to, Ms. Richardson," Roy the Professor chided. "And ideally, if we save properly for retirement, we won't have to.

"Let's assume a fictitious successful female entrepreneur was due to retire tomorrow. We'll call her . . . Cathy." Roy smiled. "Let's also assume that she has been making one hundred thousand dollars a year— considerably more than her fictitious friends and fictitious local barbershop patrons.

"Now, between her expected Social Security benefits and some interest income she will be able to generate from investing the proceeds of selling her business, Cathy expects to have an annual income of around forty thousand dollars. She would either have to live on less than half of what she was accustomed to, or dip into her ten percent fund to make up the difference.

"She wouldn't have to dip into it for just sixty thousand dollars, though. She'd have to use seven hundred and fifty thousand dollars of her fund, because it would take that amount, invested at eight percent, our standard assumed rate of return, to create a sixty-thousand-dollar annual cash flow. Suddenly, her finer-things-in-life money is being depleted dramatically. For every one dollar of needed income, twelve dollars and fifty cents must be used from the ten percent fund," Roy explained.

"Eight percent of twelve and a half being one," I calculated.

"And your dad said you were a 'math murderer,'" Roy kidded.

"I see your point, Roy, and I agree. I'm sure these two do, too," Cathy surmised correctly, motioning at Tom and me. "So, you're saying we should save ten percent and invest it for growth, and save enough separately to make up any shortfall in our post-retirement income."

"That's precisely what I'm saying. To be in truly great shape, you must do both."

"Once again, Roy, your argument makes perfect sense. Nobody could question its logic, but is it feasible?" Tom asked. "I mean, saving ten percent and saving for retirement, too, could be pretty difficult! With that on top of rent, groceries, and all the other costs of living in the nineties, I'll be cleaned out. I won't be able to leave my apartment!

"What's more, with all due respect, I don't agree with the assumption that we need to maintain our preretirement income. Everything I've read says that less income is needed in retirement. You usually don't have a mortgage anymore. Nine times out of ten, you no longer have dependent children. Your house is fully furnished. If you've saved properly, then you've stopped having to buy insurance. Obviously, expenses are way down in retirement. So, why would you need as much money then as you did in your last years of work?''

Tom had raised two very valid points. I suspected even Roy might have a tough time answering them satisfactorily.

"Let me look at your need-for-income point first. Then I'll address your isn't-this-all-a-bit-much question," Roy began, obviously pleased, not exasperated, by Tom's refusal to accept the wealthy barber's opinions as gospel.

"In most cases, several years before retirement, the mortgage has indeed been paid off, and the children have indeed moved out. So, for many, the last few years at work are characterized by good income levels and significantly reduced expenses. In all likelihood, disposable income is at its highest point ever! Upon retirement, it's no fun having to lower your standard of living because of a drop in your income. Psychologically, it's a difficult, if not traumatic, adjustment.

"If the decline in expenses happened to coincide perfectly with the date of retirement, instead of occurring earlier, maybe there wouldn't be a major problem. But it seldom happens that way. Adjusting to a significant drop in your disposable income is not my idea of a good way to start retired life, especially since it's a myth that present-day retired people spend much less money on lifestyle than their working counterparts.

"People don't retire and head straight to the rocking chair. While the rest of us are slaving away, many retirees are playing golf, taking up hobbies, traveling extensively, and participating in a myriad of other activities that have one common denominator: They cost money!

"Furthermore, you're overlooking a couple of major expenditures that sometimes arise in retirement that can be very costly—very difficult to cope with on a reduced income. Sadly, deteriorating health often goes hand-in-hand with advancing age. Any number of medical costs, including insurance, can cause your financial well-being to decline right along with your physical well-being.

"And while you probably will no longer have dependent children, what about dependent parents? As I've said many times, Americans are, for the most part, financial illiterates. You three are learning the right things to do, but most people aren't as fortunate, including most parents. Oftentimes, elderly parents need financial help from their children."

"My dad threatens me with that scenario daily." I chuckled.

"Your years in retirement should be among the best years of your life, so you owe it to yourself to do everything possible now, without crippling your current standard of living, to enable you to enjoy them to the fullest. That means saving enough money in your working years to enable you to maintain your after-tax income in retirement.

"I say 'after-tax' because, obviously, it's not so much what you make that's important—it's what you keep. In that respect, my earlier example of our fictitious Cathy needing one hundred thousand dollars in retirement to match her last year's working income was probably overstated in that some of her retirement income—her Social Security income—would receive preferential tax treatment. And, of course, she'd no longer have to make Social Security contributions.

"Finally, before I move on to Tom's question of feasibility, you must remember our old nemesis—inflation. Each year, your retirement income may remain level, but I'm afraid we can't say the same for the cost of living. As many retirees will confirm, this is no small problem. Your purchasing power can be slowly eaten away until, even though you're bringing in about the same after-tax income as during your last working year, your purchasing power has been significantly eroded. That's trouble. Big trouble. Inflation is a retiree's number one enemy. The absolute amount of your income is not the key—it's what you can buy with that income that counts."

"Meaning?" Cathy prodded.

"Meaning," Roy responded, "that having not only enough to spin off the desired annual income in retirement, but also enough extra to offset inflation's impact, is imperative—and is going to necessitate saving a great deal of money."

"That makes Tom's 'feasibility question,' as you called it, even more relevant," I offered, trying not to sound as panicky as I felt.

"The need to accumulate substantial savings for your retirement may seem intimidating, but it really isn't. Remember, you three have discovered the magic of compound interest. Once again, this time within various retirement plans, it's going to be our best friend. That shouldn't surprise you. But what might surprise you is the identity of another helpful new friend: the government."

"The government is no friend of mine, Roy," Tom scoffed. "I give it a hefty portion of everything I make, and in return, it loses my mail."

"In the case of a variety of different retirement savings vehicles, it really is your friend," Roy assured him. "As you'll see in a minute, the government often subsidizes your contributions to these plans and, perhaps even more important, allows your deposits to grow unencumbered by tax until withdrawal later in life. Remember what I said earlier about looking for the least painful ways to save for your golden years? Between the government's assistance, and savings that you will realize by purchasing term insurance instead of cash-value insurance, your qualified annual contributions to these plans will be largely financed without you having to do impossible additional saving. You will have to save some, of course, but it will be a reasonable amount. And if we use our old trick of paying ourselves first, we'll hardly notice it.

"True?" he challenged Jimmy, James Murray, and Clyde.

"True," two pronounced, over Clyde mumbling, " 'Hardly' may be a little strong."

"How exactly does the government 'subsidize' contributions?" I questioned.

"All in good time, Dave, all in good time. First, let's take a quick look at a retirement income source Tom alluded to earlier: Social Security.

"Like it or not, the government imposes what I call 'mandatory retirement-savings discipline' with its payroll tax for Social Security. It is essential, I repeat, essential, to understand that Social Security is intended to be, at best, either a safety net for retired Americans who, for whatever reasons, are in dire need of an income to subsist, or an augmentation of retirement income for those of us lucky enough to have pension income, investment assets, or both. At worst, especially for participants as young as you three, Social Security may well end up being social insecurity."

"No kidding!" Tom blurted out. "The younger guys at work are always complaining about having to pay into Social Security when a lot of articles claim that, by the time we retire, the whole thing may be bankrupt. That's a lousy deal!"

"In the eighties the system received bolstering to assure benefits for participants now in or near retirement, and Social Security currently stands on reasonably firm footing. Most experts agree that today's forty- to sixty-year-olds probably have little to worry about.

"Unfortunately, the same can't be said for your generation. Theoretically, Social Security could collapse when today's young workers retire. Politically, however, that calamity is very unlikely. Much more likely is that the rules and regulations will be altered over the years in ways that, quite frankly, no one can now forecast with any degree of certainty.

"Actually, that's not true," he mused. "Forecasters never lack for certainty; it's accuracy that is the scarce commodity."

"Just adding to Roy's point," a till-then very quiet James Murray broke in, "I read an article last week about just this topic. Every analyst quoted agreed with Roy's assertion that allowing Social Security to collapse would be political suicide. However, they also agreed that many changes are going to have to be implemented over the years in order to preserve the system.

"Remember that our aging population means there are going to be fewer and fewer people working to support more and more of us in retirement. In fact, the statistics are actually frightening. By the year 2020, some estimates have only two and a half people working for every one retiree. Fifty years ago, I believe, the ratio was over forty to one!"

"What kind of changes are they anticipating, James?" Cathy asked, as if we couldn't have guessed.

"Everything from higher payroll taxes to reduced benefits, most or all of which will probably become taxable, to the delay of the eligible retirement dates—"

"I'm sure everyone gets the idea," Roy mercifully interrupted. "Again, I remind you that the key is this: Regardless of whether or not major, and most likely negative, changes are implemented over the years, Social Security will at best remain a safety net or income augmentation. It is not your retirement plan! It is only a small part of it. Current Social Security administration projections would probably place your three retirement incomes somewhere between eleven and seventeen thousand a year, in today's dollars."

"Gee, who's the eleven thousand and who's the seventeen?" Tom joked, with a wink at Cathy.

"Remember," Roy cautioned us, "as a percentage of your current income, that represents a relatively small figure . . . forty percent, maybe less . . . thirty, perhaps—"

"Or for Cathy, about two," I facetiously sniped, before Tom could.

"Actually, all kidding aside, you're touching on a valid point. High-income types, whose annual earnings greatly exceed the maximum income used for Social-Security-calculation purposes, can find their Social Security benefits representing an almost negligible portion of their pre-retirement income. Although I'm sure you two boys are thinking, 'Hey, that's the kind of problem I wouldn't mind having,' you must remember that maintaining a high income level like Cathy's will demand a lot more in savings."

Roy went over to a drawer and pulled out a brochure, without noticing that his last point had fallen on unsympathetic ears.

"I strongly urge the three of you to contact the Social Security administration and to ask for a questionnaire entitled *Personal Earnings and Benefit Estimate Statement*. Several weeks after returning the form, you will receive a list of all your estimated benefits, including your monthly retirement check stated in today's dollars, survivor's benefits, disability benefits, a year-by-year summary of your earnings that were subject to Social Security taxes, the amount of those taxes, and other relevant figures. It's a good idea to request an updated list of benefits every couple of years, because changes to either your income level or structural changes to the system could alter the numbers fairly dramatically. There is also a three-year statute of limitations for correcting any posting errors to your account. Knowing the government, that alone should provide sufficient incentive to request the questionnaire!"

"It's clear that Social Security alone is not enough—strike that, not nearly enough—to fund our retirements. But Tom and I, like millions of others, are also members of pension plans. Between those two sources of income, we should be covered or close to it, right?"

"Not necessarily, Dave," Roy replied. "Perhaps, but not necessarily. Indeed, it's unlikely. I have several friends who work or have worked at the same plant as Tom, and they'll be the first to tell you that, although their employer-sponsored retirement plan is better than nothing, it, even combined with Social Security, is not enough to get by on. In fact, the amount they receive monthly is set at a maximum, I believe around eighteen hundred a month including their Social Security benefits. I don't deny that's an excellent start, but it's tough living on twenty thousand dollars a year when you've been accustomed to much more.

"Dave, your teachers' plan is a good one—better than Tom's, frankly. Like many retirement plans, it's a defined-benefit plan, meaning that when you retire, assuming you meet certain criteria, you will receive a monthly check based on a number of variables, the most important being your salary history and the number of years you were on the payroll. In your case, your pension income will be determined by multiplying your years of service times one and a half percent times the average of your last three years' salary. That will work out to over forty percent of your last year's working income. What's more, in retirement you'll no longer have deductions for your pension contribution and Social Security tax. Coupling those facts with the knowledge that some Social Security benefits may not be taxable leads to an inevitable conclusion—not bad, Dave . . . not bad at all."

Needless to say, I was thrilled with this news.

"You know what else, Roy?" I beamed, making no attempt to hide my enthusiasm. "My pension income is guaranteed to increase by three percent each year. Indexing, I think they call it."

"Precisely," Roy confirmed. "Indexing is certainly another fine, and I should add rare, pension feature. Most aren't indexed and won't increase each year to either fully or partially offset the impact of inflation.

"As I pointed out earlier," Roy continued, "inflation is most pensioners' number one enemy. A non-indexed pension's purchasing power dwindles with startling speed. Even a partially indexed pension like yours, Dave, capped

107

at three percent, can be overwhelmed by an extended period of high inflation like we saw in the early eighties."

I should have known that the string of good news couldn't go on forever.

"So what you're saying," I attempted to summarize, "is that even someone like me, who has a generous retirement program, should do some additional saving. One: to make up for the shortfall between my last working year's after-tax income and the after-tax retirement income provided by my retirement program and Social Security. And two: to help offset the ravages of inflation."

To say this was the most insightful thought of my financial career would be a gross understatement. Even Roy looked shocked.

"That's exactly what I'm saying," he stammered, "although I don't believe I've ever said it so eloquently.

"It's imperative that everyone who is a member of a company retirement plan contact his or her personnel department to determine what benefits can be expected, at what age they can begin to be drawn, what the survivor benefits are, whether the retirement benefits are affected by Social Security benefits, and what the vesting schedule is. Vesting refers to an employee being able to retain his or her retirement benefits if a change of employer occurs. When those questions are answered, the vast majority of people, with the exception of some high-level executives, will recognize the need to do at least a moderate amount of supplementary saving for retirement —even those with generous pension programs.

"Of course, people like Cathy, who aren't members of pension plans, or like Jimmy, whose, frankly, is terrible, must do a great deal of saving.

"The question obviously is, 'What are the best vehicles to use to accomplish our goals?'"

"That's why we're here, Roy," came Cathy's polite reminder.

"You may not know the vehicles' specific names or subtleties, but you already know our selection criteria."

Nothing sprang to my mind, as Tom replaced me in the chair.

"We do?" Cathy said with puzzlement.

Roy remained silent.

Finally, lightning struck. "We want to choose vehicles that enable us to attain our long-term savings goals but which, at the same time, require the smallest ongoing sacrifices. 'Building for the future without killing the present,' to quote one of America's great financial minds." Cathy repeated Tom's earlier remark to wild applause from the gallery.

"That point bears repeating," Roy said solemnly, when the bravos died down. "As we examine a number of the retirement-savings alternatives, two questions should constantly be going through your minds. One: Is this alternative available to me? Two: Will it help me achieve my savings goals in a less costly or painful manner than the other choices?

"I should point out now that it is not my intention to cover all the rules and regulations for each available plan. That would take days. However, there are several excellent books that you should consult, a couple of which I'll recommend before you leave today.

"Instead, my objective is simply to look at the major pros and cons of some of the main alternatives, and to give you some general guidance—to point you in the right direction, if you will.

"Let's start with the best-known of all retirement plans: the IRA."

"I have one of those," Cathy announced, "although it's not very big, because I can only put in two thousand a year, right?"

"That is correct and, because of that restriction, an IRA might not be the most suitable savings choice for you. In fact, because of other restrictions, it may not be the most suitable choice for any of you. However, I'll let you make your own decisions after our discussion.

"IRA stands for Individual Retirement Account. IRAs are really nothing more than personal retirement funds set up by people who have earned income. You must have earned income, by the way, to open an IRA—earned through wages, salary, self-employment income, professional fees, bonuses, tips, alimony—"

"Alimony!" Cathy and Tom exclaimed in disbelief.

"Hey, believe me—alimony is often the hardest-earned income anyone will ever come by." Roy chuckled.

"What about rent?" Tom, the new real-estate mogul, questioned.

"No. Rental income, interest, dividends, and most income earned from sources outside the U.S. are all excluded.

"Contributions are restricted to two thousand dollars or one hundred percent of your earned income, whichever is less. Mind you, one-income couples' annual contribution can total twenty-two hundred and fifty dollars, as long as no more than two thousand is allocated to either spouse.

"A great thing about IRAs, in fact, a great thing about all of the alternatives we're about to discuss, is that once your money is in the plan, it is allowed to grow on a tax-deferred basis until withdrawn."

"A second major advantage," a somewhat-informed Cathy ventured, "is that the two-thousand-dollar contribution is tax-deductible!"

"May be tax-deductible," Roy corrected her. "If neither you nor your spouse, if you have one, is covered by any type of retirement plan, profit-sharing arrangement, or Keogh plan, then one or both of you, whatever the case may be, may make a tax-deductible IRA contribution no matter how much money you're making. If retirement plan coverage exists, you can still fully deduct IRA contributions if you're single and making less than an adjusted gross income of twenty-five thousand a year, or if you're married and your joint adjusted gross income is less than forty thousand a year. Once your income exceeds those levels, the deductible portion of your IRA contributions drops from one hundred percent to zero at the rate of ten percent per thousand of excess income."

"What?"

"It's not as tricky as it sounds," Roy consoled me. "If you and Sue were making a combined income of forty-eight thousand a year, how much of your two-thousand-dollar IRA contribution could you deduct?"

"Well," I hazarded, "that's eight thousand above the IRA threshold for couples . . . ten percent reduction per thousand . . . leaves twenty percent . . . of my maximum two thousand contribution . . . I could deduct only four hundred dollars . . . and so could Sue."

"Exactly. Tom, you try one. Let's say—"

"Thanks anyway, Roy. I think I've got it," Tom said disdainfully.

"So, Roy, should I contribute two thousand dollars knowing only four hundred will be deductible?" I pressed on eagerly.

"That depends on whether, after evaluating your other alternatives, your IRA contribution represents your best choice—"

"That is, your least painful choice," I stopped Roy.

"You're catching on, Dave . . . slowly, mind you, but you're catching on. I'll talk more later about the advantages and disadvantages of non-deductible contributions."

"Roy, the contributions I've made have been fully deductible because I'm not a participant in any other type of retirement program. I'm thinking of taking a year off sometime fairly soon to travel. Wouldn't it make sense to cash out my IRA at that time, because I'll be in a lower tax bracket that year?"

Cathy's idea made sense to me.

"That's good thinking," he congratulated her. "However, withdrawing funds from your IRA prior to age fifty-nine-and-a-half is usually a mistake—both from a mathematical and from a common sense point of view.

"You see, if you withdraw money from your IRA prior to that age, you don't just pay tax on that amount. You

111

also pay a ten percent penalty tax. This penalty doesn't apply if you're totally and permanently disabled or if the IRA is converted to equal payments over your life expectancy—neither being the case with you, Cathy.

"In addition to having to pay the standard tax and the penalty tax, you also lose one of the major benefits of an IRA: The withdrawn money can no longer grow on a tax-deferred, compounding basis. That hurts!

"Finally, and just as important, in the highly unlikely event that your fancy footwork is a good mathematical move, from a common sense standpoint it's still questionable. You'll be defeating the prime purpose of IRAs: a savings vehicle for your retirement! Trust me, you'll find small consolation as an impoverished retiree in the fact that many years ago by cashing out a portion of your IRA holdings you saved a few hundred dollars that you probably ended up blowing anyway."

"Assuming I decide an IRA should play a role in my retirement planning, how do you suggest I invest it?" Tom forged ahead.

"As with all investments, your decision should take into account potential rewards, your risk tolerance, and the relevant time frame."

I truly hate vague answers like that.

"So, for investors as young as we are, mutual funds selected using the same techniques we learned two months ago would make a great deal of sense," Cathy reasoned. "A properly selected global equity mutual fund offers excellent potential rewards and minimal risk over the long term. What could be longer term than our IRAs, for Pete's sake?"

"Hey, watch your language!" Clyde scolded my sister.

"I strongly agree with your comments," Roy said warmly. "Everything you said makes perfect sense, and I congratulate you for emphasizing the terms 'properly selected' and 'long term.' Those considerations remain vital, as they did with your ten percent savings. Despite my strong agreement, though, I must say that one place

112

an ultraconservative investor—a loaner—can survive and prosper is within a tax-deferred vehicle such as an IRA. Because loanership investments, like CDs—certificates of deposit—are allowed to compound, unencumbered by tax, year after year, they can perform quite admirably. Again, I don't think that over the long term they have a snowball's chance in hell of outperforming a well-selected mutual fund, but they can perform respectably."

"Our old friend, compound interest," James Murray joined in. "Nowhere is she given more chance to shine than within a tax-deferred vehicle. The combination of time and compound interest is more powerful than a locomotive, a nuclear reaction, or even a Cecil Fielder home run. John D. Rockefeller often spoke of the magic of compound interest. He once said, 'If you want to become really wealthy, you must have your money work for you. The amount you get paid for your personal effort is relatively small compared with the amount you can earn by having your money make money.' He knew whereof he spoke."

After an appropriately dramatic pause, James continued.

"With all due respect to our leader here, I have eschewed his advice in this one area. Over the years, I have placed the majority of my tax-deferred investments in CDs, bonds, and the like. Only when the U.S. stock markets have declined for two consecutive years have I invested in equity mutual funds. This extremely conservative strategy has served me well," James boasted.

This particular point, although I'm sure a good one, was lost on me. I was still wondering what "eschew" meant.

"No offense, Roy, but I think I may follow James's lead and invest my tax-deferred money primarily in loanership investments. You yourself said it's the one place a loaner can prosper, and with me already investing my ten percent savings in mutual funds, it makes sense from a diversification standpoint, too. Plus, without a pension, I may sleep better at night knowing that my retirement funds aren't subject to the ups and downs of the markets."

Heresy, I thought. After all Roy had done for us, how could Cathy possibly disagree with him?

"Thirty years from now, I'm sure, repeat, *sure*, that you'll regret your decision, but I do agree that your points make sense—especially the one about being able to sleep at night. That's an important part of any investment decision.

"We still have a number of things to cover, so let me end our discussion of IRAs with some very important tips. One: Make every effort to make your IRA contributions as early in the year as possible. Just because you're allowed to wait until April fifteenth of the following year doesn't mean that you should. If you have the money sitting around, get it out of a fully taxable situation and into a tax-deferred situation ASAP. Not only will contributing early year after year eventually increase your IRA value by tens of thousands of dollars, but it will also rid you of the temptation to blow the money on something frivolous! And, if you're going to go the fund route, why not set up a preauthorized checking arrangement again? Forced savings—you can't beat it.

"Two: Dave, and you two once you're married, name your spouse as beneficiary of your IRA. Then, in the event of your death, your IRA can be rolled over into your spouse's IRA with no tax ramifications. That is not the case if your plan is left to your estate or to a third party.

"Three: If you want to follow James's example of placing most of your tax-deferred monies in CDs and comparable investments, keep this strategy in mind: Open up a self-administered IRA, that is, an IRA that allows you to manage your own investments, and then buy a monthly-pay, five-year CD. Then, each month, buy an equity fund with the interest—all within the self-administered plan, of course. It's beautiful—all your capital is guaranteed, yet you're still reaping the benefits of ownership, dollar cost averaging, professional money management . . . the works. It's tidy—there are no small amounts of money left sitting idly by. It's easy—twenty minutes of work a year, and no complicated investment decisions. Essentially, what you're doing is compounding your CD interest into ownership. It's a great compromise!''

I could tell by the expression on Tom's and Cathy's faces that I wasn't the only one who found this idea appealing.

"Four: Regardless of which tax-deferred vehicle you select, IRA or other, start contributing now! I can't stress that enough.

"Two twenty-two-year-old twins decide to start saving for retirement. One opens an IRA, invests two thousand dollars a year for six years, and then stops. His IRA compounds at twelve percent a year . . . very good. The second twin procrastinates and doesn't open an IRA until the seventh year—the year his brother stopped. The second twin then contributes two thousand a year for thirty-seven years. He, too, earns a rate of twelve percent a year. At age sixty-five, they go out for dinner to compare their IRA holdings. The second twin, who is fully aware that his brother stopped contributing thirty-seven years earlier, is confident that his IRA will be worth at least ten times as much. What do you think, Cathy?''

"I think he's wrong . . . or you wouldn't be telling us the story," was her clever rationale.

"Yeah, yeah," Roy laughed. "At age sixty-five, they would both have approximately one million two hundred thousand dollars.''

Despite Cathy's glib response, the significance of Roy's example was not lost on any of us. It was hard-hitting testimony to the benefits of starting one's saving early.

"All right. Let's look at some other savings alternatives. I'm holding forth even longer than last month," Roy conceded, glancing at his watch.

"One second, Roy. If we decide to, where should we buy our IRAs?"

"Banks, brokerage firms, mutual fund companies, insurance agents, and more. It seems that everyone is selling IRAs. To select the one best suited to you is going to take some reading. A little basic research never hurt anyone. Make sure you shop the market, as rates offered, fees, commissions, et cetera, can vary a great deal from one IRA to the next. Even after you've established an IRA, it still doesn't hurt to keep an eye open, because there are transfer and rollover provisions that allow you to move your IRA dollars without triggering a tax liability."

Although I'd hoped that Roy would have been a bit more specific, I wasn't too disappointed. Much to my amazement, in three short months I had reached the point where I didn't mind doing some elementary financial research.

"If you are self-employed, even on a part-time basis, or if you're in partnership, an excellent retirement vehicle is available to you: the Keogh plan. So, who should be paying attention to this section?"

Only Cathy raised her hand.

"I asked that deceptively simple question for a reason," Roy went on. "For some unknown reason, a great number of people equate 'self-employed' with 'self-employed full-time.' That can be a costly misconception. Tom, you mentioned several months ago that you had made a few thousand last year driving a delivery truck occasionally for a friend. That is income from self-employment, so you, too, qualify for a Keogh plan. And Dave, you should be ashamed for not raising your hand! Aren't you forgetting a certain intelligent and attractive woman living with you who is very successfully self-employed? As a freelancer, Sue generates significant self-employment income."

Good point.

"Where does the name Keogh come from?" I wondered.

"Who cares?"

116

"I'm inclined to agree with Tom, Dave. The history of the plan's name is unimportant . . . the potential benefits of utilizing a Keogh are not, the major ones being, like the IRA, tax-deductibility of contributions and tax-deferred growth. However, unlike the IRA, Keoghs allow for contributions far in excess of two thousand dollars a year. For people like Cathy and me, that increased allowable-contribution level is vital to our retirement planning.

"How much you can contribute to a Keogh plan is dependent upon the type of plan you choose. The majority of us select a defined-contribution plan. Your retirement benefits in this type of plan will be dependent upon the amounts you have contributed over the years and how well you have invested the funds.

"There are two types of defined-contribution plans. The first is a money-purchase plan to which, quite simply, you contribute based on a fixed percentage of your income and your employees' income."

"Your employees' income?" Cathy repeated.

"Yes, Cathy, that is one negative associated with setting up a Keogh plan. Generally, you must include your full-time employees who fall within certain parameters in your plan. So, you must contribute to their retirement accounts. Of course, your contributions to their accounts are deductible. Even so, the cost of including these employees may eliminate your personal tax savings for your own contributions. Increased goodwill will have, I'm sure, a slight balancing effect, but you can't take goodwill to the bank. Weigh such a situation carefully."

"None of us has any employees. Not even Cathy," I remarked.

"That makes it easy," Roy acknowledged. "Now back to money-purchase plans. You are allowed to contribute twenty-five percent of your earned income or thirty thousand dollars, whichever is less. Mind you, that statement is a bit misleading, because earned income, for the purpose

117

of calculating contributions, is defined as net income from self-employment *less* the Keogh contribution. So, really, you can only contribute twenty percent of your actual net income or thirty thousand, whichever is less."

"Only? Are you kidding? That's great!" Cathy exclaimed. "I can solve all my retirement-savings problems with one plan—a Keogh."

"That's right," James Murray agreed. "These really are great opportunities. One problem with money-purchase plans, though, that doesn't affect you 'employee-less' self-employed, is that you must contribute your established percentage to your employees' accounts even if you show a loss. Obviously, that may not be ideal."

"I'd forgotten that, James," Roy admitted, "but it's an important point and it's the reason why, for some self-employed people, the second type of defined-contribution plan may make more sense: the profit-sharing plan. As the name indicates, that type of plan's contributions are based on a percentage of profits, with the advantage of allowing you to alter the percentage each year or, if need be, of not contributing at all. This flexibility is attractive to a lot of self-employed people, especially those with employees.

"Of course, everything has its drawbacks, and the major one for profit-sharing plans is that your maximum contribution is limited to fifteen percent of net income rather than twenty-five. Again, because of the manner in which net income is defined for purposes of deductions, that fifteen percent is more accurately stated as just above thirteen percent of actual net income."

"If it's your desire to put aside more than thirteen percent, but you're apprehensive about committing to higher contributions, you can set up two plans—one of each type—as long as the combined contributions don't cross the twenty-percent-of-your-net-self-employment-income threshold," James advised us.

"Or thirty thousand dollars," Cathy recalled.

"Another good idea, James. In addition to the two types of defined-contribution plans, there is also a defined-benefit plan," Roy continued. "This type of Keogh allows you to contribute up to levels that will enable you to achieve an income in retirement equal to an average of your earnings in your three consecutive highest-paid years, to a maximum of around a hundred thousand per year. That amount will be indexed each year. Your contributions will be based on your current income, how many years you have left until retirement, life expectancy, and other actuarial concerns.

"This type of plan can, on occasion, be a very prudent choice. For example, if you have few years left until retirement, a defined-benefit plan will enable you to make significantly larger annual contributions than either of the defined-contribution plans. However, these plans are much more expensive to set up and administer than the other alternatives.

"It is imperative, I repeat, *imperative*, that before you set up your Keogh plan, you consult a qualified accountant, attorney, or financial planner for advice. Deciding which type of plan best suits your needs will be greatly aided by the advice of an experienced, knowledgeable professional.

"I have just a couple more Keogh pointers before we move on.

"One: Although Keogh contributions, like IRA contributions, need not be made until April fifteenth of the following year or, at the very latest, the extended filing deadline of August fifteenth, still the Keogh plan must be set up by December thirty-first of the year for which the deduction is claimed. If you're going to set up a Keogh, get moving.

"Two: The advice I gave you regarding IRA investing also applies to Keogh investing: Start now in order to take maximum advantage of compound interest; don't withdraw early and therefore subject yourself to penalties *and* to opportunity cost; contribute early in the year, if possible; use a comfortable combination of CDs, other secure loanership investments, and well-selected equity mutual funds; and, finally, do some reading. Any questions?''

''Do you think it's important for Dave and me to seek some professional guidance, or just Cathy?'' Tom asked.

''All of you. Selecting the proper type of plan and plan structure is very important. It'll pay big dividends in the long run to make a small investment in expert advice beforehand.''

''I know you're eager to move on, Roy, but you may want to mention SEPs,'' James Murray intervened.

''SEP stands for Simplified Employee Pension. Basically, that's a pension plan in which both the employer and the employees make deductible contributions to individuals' retirement accounts—IRAs. Deductions are restricted to fifteen percent of income or thirty thousand dollars—again, whichever is less. SEPs involve less paperwork than Keoghs, a drawback to Keoghs that I should have mentioned, and are usually less expensive to set up. The SEP contributions, though, with the fifteen percent maximum, are potentially not as high.

''To determine which plan is best for you, guess what you do?''

''Seek the advice of a professional,'' we chimed in unison.

''As you know, the vast majority of people are not self-employed, and therefore can't set up either a Keogh plan or an SEP. How do these people set out to create a pool of capital to augment their Social Security benefits, and pension checks, if any?

''IRAs are one previously discussed alternative, but for a growing number of Americans the most attractive choice may be a 401(k) plan.''

''Hey, I'm pretty sure we have one of those at work,'' Tom piped up. ''But I'm not sure I know exactly what it is.''

"It's a retirement savings plan that, like the vehicles we've already examined, allows you to make deductible contributions that will grow on a tax-deferred basis. Unlike the other vehicles, this one often involves employers matching your contributions to some degree. Remember our edict to seek the least painful way to save? This is probably it!"

"Great! Who should we talk to? Our personnel departments?"

"Sorry, Dave, the Board of Education doesn't offer a 401(k), but your idea of talking to your personnel department was a good one. All employees should do that to find out whether a 401(k) plan is available and, if so, the important details of it."

"What are the contribution limits?" an interested Tom inquired.

"The law allows you to have a salary reduction of approximately eight thousand five hundred dollars directed to a 401(k) and that contribution is not taxed. That limit, by the way, is indexed to inflation and, therefore, is increased each year. In addition, your employer as well may, and as I mentioned earlier, usually does, contribute on your behalf. The employer's contribution is also subject to limits, of course . . . generous limits, though. How much you'll actually be allowed to contribute will depend not only on the government-dictated limit but also on your own corporation's parameters. For example, they may allow you to contribute only up to a certain percentage of your income. Moreover, contribution limits may also be affected by your involvement in other retirement plans such as SEPs. Your personnel department would definitely be able to clarify the specifics for you."

"I'm sure most of your investment advice for IRAs and Keoghs holds true here, too, Roy: Don't withdraw early and therefore face penalties, and all that stuff. But from your brief description, it sounds as though my company may control some of the investment decisions. True?"

"To some extent, yes, though companies normally give employees a number of choices. You'll usually be able to choose from among a CD-type savings plan, a variety of mutual funds, and often a plan that invests in stock of your company. I'd be somewhat leery of that last choice. Remember, when you're investing in the stock market, diversification is essential to your success. It's tough to sleep at night with all your eggs in one basket."

Tom looked perplexed. "You mentioned choosing from a variety of mutual funds. Did you mean from a limited variety selected by our company, or any fund we want?"

"Unfortunately, the former. Well, 'unfortunately' may not be the right word, because it's in your company's best interests to choose a reputable group by applying the same selection criteria that you would. Nevertheless, you may want to investigate their choices, and if you're uncomfortable with them, go the CD-type savings plan route.

"401(k)s are, for the most part, excellent deals, and are becoming more and more popular. The matching provision can really help!" Roy summarized.

"That's great for Tom, Roy, but what about me? I realize my wife can open a Keogh, but it seems that nothing is available to me. No 401(k), no Keogh, no SEP, no fully deductible IRA . . . C'mon," I pleaded.

"Good news, my friend, good news," Roy assured me. "As a teacher, you probably qualify for participation in a 403(b) retirement plan. It, too, is a salary-reduction plan, like a 401(k). With the 403(b), your deductible contributions are invested in a tax-sheltered annuity.

"Again, it's crucial to talk to your personnel department. They'll have all the pertinent information, including your investment options and allowable contribution limits.

"I know that I'm nagging you, but seeing your personnel departments to learn about the alternatives available to you is one of the most important steps in retirement planning. It's impossible to decide which is the least painful alternative if you don't even know all the alternatives.

"By next month I want each of you to have paid a visit to your personnel department and to have learned what plans are there for the choosing."

"Shouldn't be hard for me," Cathy said with a grin.

"I also want you to do a bit of reading. There are several excellent books that cover saving for retirement. Two that I highly recommend are J. K. Lasser's *Tax-Sheltered Retirement Plans* and the very-easy-to-read *Smart Money* by Ken and Daria Dolan.

"Today's lesson, combined with a minimal amount of reading and a trip down the hall at your place of work, can make a great difference to your retirement years.

"You see, this stuff is not that tough!" Roy concluded.

"I know we've been here forever, Roy, but I still have one question." I ignored a look from my anxious-to-golf best friend. "You promised earlier that you would comment on the merits of non-deductible IRA contributions. Well?"

"I'm glad you didn't let me forget that. There are a number of available investments that allow you to make *non-deductible* contributions to a tax-deferred vehicle. In these vehicles, clearly you are receiving only one of the two government incentives associated with those plans we discussed earlier. That is, your money is still growing on a tax-deferred basis, but you don't get to deduct your contributions from your taxable income. Assuming that these vehicles can sometimes be wise choices, under what circumstances would you consider them?" Roy tested us.

"When none of the other plans is available to us . . . or when we have reached the deductibility limits of our chosen plans and want to do further retirement saving," Cathy noted without missing a beat.

"Precisely. For example, Dave making a non-deductible IRA contribution without making his maximum allowable deductible contribution to his 403(b) plan would be a debatable move. But if you have none of those alternatives available, then, yes, non-deductible IRA contributions and tax-deferred annuity purchases may make sense."

"Tax-deferred annuity?" Tom repeated with raised eyebrows.

"Basically, it's an insurance-company-issued product that allows an investor to make non-deductible contributions to an annuity product and receive the benefits of tax-deferred growth and a wide range of specific investment choices. Unfortunately, the fees for this type of product are sometimes very high . . . very high.

"And always remember our golden rule: Choose the least painful alternative available!

"My parting comment," Roy said, to Tom's evident relief, "is that you three have come a long way. You're asking intelligent questions. You're applying what you're learning. You're on your way to becoming very wealthy. Congratulations!"

Cathy acted as our spokesperson. "We owe it all to you, Roy. We can't thank you enough."

"Well, as a matter of fact, you can," Roy informed us, as we paid for our long-since-completed haircuts. "Give me your tickets for tomorrow's Tigers game."

"No way!" Tom roared. "Nothing's worth that much! But you'll be our first guest when we get season tickets a few years from now."

Chapter 7

Home, Sweet Home

"WELL, IF IT ISN'T JACK Nicklaus," Jimmy bellowed, as I entered Roy's with Cathy and Tom. "When did they add Port Huron to the tour?"

"The Golden Bear! This is such an honor! Can I have your autograph?" James Murray gushed. "It's for my wife, of course!"

"Did you win a trophy or something?" Roy wondered.

"Slow down, guys," I replied. "I feel like I'm on *Meet the Press*. No, Port Huron is still not on the circuit. Yes, you can have my autograph. And yes, Roy, I won a trophy."

"What club did you hit?" asked Clyde, offering me a doughnut.

"Yes, let's relive the whole event," Tom cut in sarcastically. "Hey, I've only heard the details two hundred times . . . It is a sunny, windless Tuesday afternoon as Dave Richardson steps up to the third tee. One hundred and sixty yards stretch before him. Water lies on the left. A bunker lurks on the right. Perils abound. Dave laughs in the face of danger, pulls out a seven iron, takes a smooth, sweet swing and . . . the ball rockets straight ahead . . . takes one small skip. . . and lands right in the hole.

"The crowd—consisting of Mr. Richardson and me—goes crazy. So does Dave. He doesn't just get a hole-in-one. Oh, no. He also gets a career-low score of seventy-three. And in the process he takes his closest and most loyal friend, as well as his own flesh and blood, for every cent they have. Of course, we made him buy us, and everyone else in the clubhouse, a drink. History was made that fateful afternoon. It was an honor to be a part of it, in my own small, humble way."

"Jealousy rears its ugly head," I laughed.

"When are you heading back to Ann Arbor, Jack? For that matter, when's Mrs. Nicklaus due?" Roy inquired.

"We leave Monday. I can't believe that five weeks have come and gone," I answered, shaking my head. "Sue's due in a few weeks—September fifth, to be exact."

"You must be getting pretty excited."

"'Excited' is not the word. I can hardly sleep at night. Not only are we about to have a baby, but we're also going to buy a house sometime in the next month or so. Parenthood, home ownership, and an amazing Tiger drive to the pennant, all in one month. Unbelievable!

"You know, it's funny. I'm more nervous about buying a house than I am about being a father. How hard can changing diapers be? It's the thought of borrowing eighty thousand dollars that makes me a little queasy."

"C'mon, Dave. People say buying a house is the smartest thing they've ever done . . . the best investment of their lives," Tom consoled me.

"You'll never regret buying a house, Dave. I'll guarantee it," James Murray affirmed confidently.

"It's true," Cathy agreed. "You know what they say. 'Renting is like throwing your money away.'"

"What a coincidence! Home ownership is today's subject. Actually, it's not such a coincidence," Roy admitted. "I was going to discuss saving and the use of credit, but I don't see any harm in delaying that until next month.

"Let me start by saying that whoever the ubiquitous 'they' are who say 'renting is like throwing your money away' aren't accurate. I've read that opinion in several well-known financial planning guides, and I just don't know where the authors are coming from. Paying rent is no more throwing your money away than buying food or clothing is. You need shelter. It's one of the three basic necessities of life. Renting is one way to acquire that shelter and, in some cases, it's a very intelligent way.

"I'll let you in on another secret. The reason the vast majority of homeowners say that their house is the best investment they've ever made is simple: It's usually the only investment they've ever made. My customers are always saying to me, 'Yep, Roy, my house is the best investment the wife and I have ever made.' I ask them, 'What else have you invested in?' 'Hmm,' they reply, 'we bought some old stamps one time . . . oh, and a stock on the Denver exchange.' I'm sure you get my drift. The fact—"

"Hold on, Roy," I interrupted. "You're not trying to tell us that you don't believe in home ownership, are you? I've never heard of anyone who lost money through home ownership. And you get to live there rent-free, too."

"No, Dave, I'm not saying that I don't believe in home ownership. But I am saying that there are some widely held misconceptions about the investment merits of owning a home. Do I believe you should own a home, Dave? Yes. But do I believe everyone should own a home? No!

"As I said a moment ago, along with food and clothing, shelter is one of life's three essentials. Everyone needs shelter and it can be obtained in only two ways: You can rent it, or you can own it."

"I want to own," I interjected emphatically. "Mom and Dad bought our house thirty years ago for fifteen thousand dollars. Today it's worth eighty-five thousand. That's pretty darn good, isn't it?"

"What rate of return does that represent?" Roy asked me.

"I don't know. It's grown over fivefold in thirty years. It must be a pretty high rate of return," I reasoned.

"Just under six percent. A six percent average annual compound rate of return. Is that 'pretty high'?" Roy questioned.

"No, I suppose not. But they also got to live there rent-free all those years," I pointed out.

"Now you're getting to the heart of the matter, Dave. How much of a down payment did your parents make?"

"I remember Dad telling me that they put down twenty percent. So, that's . . . "

"Three thousand dollars," Tom rescued me.

"Leaving them a mortgage of twelve thousand dollars. The monthly payment on that mortgage would have been approximately equal to what it would have cost them to rent a similar home," Roy stated.

"So, in reality," he continued, "they didn't turn fifteen thousand dollars into eighty-five thousand. They turned three thousand into eighty-five thousand."

"You've lost me," Cathy confessed, shaking her head.

"Your parents invested only three thousand of their own money. The rest was borrowed. And, although they obviously had to pay the money back, the costs of doing so were roughly equal to what their rent would have been had they been tenants in the same house— meaning that buying the house really only cost them the down payment.

"Look at Tom's real-estate deal. The place cost sixty-four thousand dollars, with the mortgage being for forty-six thousand. The monthly mortgage payment, including taxes, is around five hundred and twenty dollars. That amount is being covered by the rent. Therefore, Tom and his brother's only cost is the down payment.

"Your own home is really no different, except you are your own tenant. Your mortgage costs are being covered by your own rent—rent you would have had to pay anyway," Roy concluded.

"You're saying that our parents didn't turn fifteen thousand dollars into eighty-five thousand; they turned three thousand into eighty-five thousand. Right?" I repeated Roy's earlier statements to confirm my understanding.

"Precisely, Dave. And that represents an average annual compound return of . . . around eleven and three quarters percent." Roy's answer was aided by James Murray's watch-calculator.

"Is that all?" Cathy wondered.

"Is that all?" Roy echoed, with a look of dismay. "Hey, that's not bad, especially when you consider the other advantages of home ownership."

"I didn't mean it that way," Cathy defended herself. "I realize eleven and three quarters percent is a more-than-decent rate of return. It's just that I thought it would take a lot more than that rate to turn three thousand into eighty-five thousand over thirty years."

"The magic of compound interest never ceases to amaze," Jimmy added.

"That is a good rate of return, Roy," Tom resumed. "Especially because, as you said, there are other benefits, too. The interest portion of your mortgage payments is tax-deductible, isn't it? And the whole time you're making all that money, you get to enjoy living in the comfort of your own home. No wonder people say their house is the best investment they've ever made!"

"Your points are well taken, Tom," Roy began. "Your mortgage interest is fully deductible and, what's more, you are also able to claim a deduction for your property taxes. Those are tremendous tax breaks."

"In addition," James Murray leapt in, "there is another important tax-related reason to own your own home. When you sell your principal residence there is a deferral of the capital-gains tax if, within two years, you buy another that costs at least as much as the one you sold. Generally, you can take advantage of this provision no more than once every two years, although if you're moving for a job-related reason that may not be the case.

"Not only is there the 'rollover rule' I just stated, but there is also available a once-in-a-lifetime exclusion from the tax on any capital gain up to one hundred and twenty-five thousand dollars arising from the sale of your principal residence if you're fifty-five or older and if you meet certain other conditions."

"By the confused looks on your faces, I can tell an example may be in order," the always-observant Roy volunteered. "Let's say that Tom purchased a principal residence for seventy thousand dollars. Ten years from now he sells it for one hundred and forty grand. Normally, the sale of such a capital asset would, unfortunately, trigger an immediate capital-gains tax liability. So, in this case, Tom would expect to pay tax on the gain of seventy thousand. However, as James pointed out, when the capital asset is your principal residence, then the unique, and I should add, welcome, 'rollover rule' is available to save the day. To defer his tax liability, all Tom would have to do, sometime within two years of the sale of his first home, is buy another principal residence worth at least one hundred and forty thousand dollars."

"What if he bought a house for one hundred thousand dollars?"

"He'd have to pay tax on the forty-thousand-dollar gain," Roy explained. "It's really quite straightforward."

"If Tom had been over fifty-five at the time of the sale, then no capital-gains tax would be payable because of the one-hundred-and-twenty-five-thousand-dollar lifetime exclusion," my sister added, flaunting her grasp of the topic.

"Well done, Cathy," Roy commended her. "There are two brief tips I want to offer. One: Keep good records of your remodeling and improvement costs. Those expenditures can be added to the cost base of your house, thereby lowering your capital gain on a sale. Two: Remember that the once-in-a-lifetime exemption is just that—once in a lifetime. If, after turning fifty-five, you were to sell your house and become a renter, it may not be a prudent move to claim the exemption if your resulting taxable capital gain is substantially under the one-hundred-

and-twenty-five-thousand-dollar exclusion limit and if there's a chance you might become a homeowner again. It may be better to save the once-in-a-lifetime exemption in case you can take better advantage of it later."

"The lifetime exclusion aside, it seems to me that, the way these rules are designed, the government is not only promoting home ownership but also promoting perpetual home ownership. In an attempt to avoid capital-gains taxes, most people may never sell and move to an apartment or smaller house," Tom logically concluded.

"An extremely important point and one I'll discuss further in a few minutes," Roy promised.

"The tax incentives associated with home ownership do indeed make it an appealing investment. Those benefits, combined with real estate's finest quality—*leveragibility*—make owning your own home unbeatable," James Murray stated in a very matter-of-fact tone.

"Leveragibility?" Cathy and I said simultaneously.

"That's an investment term coined by one of the finest financial minds of our time—me. Leveragibility applies to an investment that has not only the ability to be leveraged, that is, to be borrowed against, but also has the ability to produce an income to offset the costs of being leveraged. You see, not only can you borrow against the value of your real-estate property, that is, mortgage it, you can also usually cover the costs of that borrowing with the rental income. It's that leveragibility that makes real estate the greatest investment of all time," replied a very convincing James Murray.

"I really think you should be on late-night TV peddling seminar kits, James," Roy laughed. "I do agree that 'leveragibility,' as you call it, is the reason that real estate is such an attractive investment. As I showed with our earlier examples, the fact that rental income can offset borrowing costs means that a relatively small investment, the down payment, can grow dramatically even if real-estate values only grow by six percent a year. Imagine if they were to grow by more than that."

"You just can't beat owning your house, " James Murray argued. "In addition to the benefits we've already discussed, there's the pride-in-ownership factor. It really does feel good to go home every night to your own house . . . a great source of pride . . . a big part of the great American dream.

"Home ownership, I'm surprised that Roy hasn't mentioned, is also one of the best forced-saving methods around. You have to make your mortgage payment or else the bank gets very annoyed. Roy once said that he feels this may be one of the most important attributes of buying over renting: the building of equity through compulsory monthly payments."

It's not hard to see why James Murray does so well in business. He believes in what he's selling.

"Leveragibility, tax incentives, forced savings, and the joys of owning your own home—why would anybody rent? Here's an even better question: Why am I renting?" Tom wondered aloud.

"Despite everything we've said, there are some legitimate reasons for renting, Tom," Roy assured him. "For some people, it may occasionally be better to rent than to own.

"There was one iffy assumption in our previous examples, but none of you picked up on it. When I was speaking of your parents' monthly mortgage payment, I said that it would have been approximately the same as the cost to rent a similar home. James and I maintained that assumption of equality between a mortgage payment and rent throughout our discussion. The prob—"

"I see it," Tom leapt in. "I definitely see it! You've assumed that the place you choose to rent will be similar to the residence you choose not to buy. That may not be the case. In fact, it rarely is the case. Look at me. I'm not about to rent a two-bedroom house. My apartment is more than sufficient."

"You seem to be developing an excellent financial mind, Tom," Roy said sincerely. "Do you two understand the significance of his comment? For a lot of individuals, the assumption that a potential mortgage payment will be roughly the same as their rental payment is a false one. Tom's case epitomizes the situation in which many single people find themselves. They're looking at rent of four hundred dollars, or a mortgage payment of hundreds of dollars more. Suddenly, *renting versus buying* is no longer *apples versus apples*. Yes, home ownership still provides a solid investment vehicle fueled by leveragibility and a preferential tax treatment. But it may cost several hundred dollars a month more than renting, even with the tax relief. That's a lot of money. What if Tom rented all his life and added that multi-hundred difference to his ten percent fund? How do you think he would fare?''

Roy's point was a good one. The three of us were by now fully aware of the power of compound interest.

''The hole I see in your argument, Roy, is that you are assuming people will invest the difference between the cost of renting and that of buying. Most won't,'' James Murray charged.

''I'll grant you that home ownership is the ultimate forced-saving program, and that is one of its other big benefits,'' Roy conceded. ''But I believe that, through paying oneself first, a renter can discipline him or herself to save some of the difference in cost between renting and owning. I say 'some' because it may not be necessary to save the entire difference to come out ahead.''

''Why do you say that?''

''Look at the homeowner for a second. He or she is thrilled that his or her—''

''Its?'' I suggested helpfully.

''Good idea, Dave. 'Its' home value is rising but, in most cases, that increased value does 'it' little good. If 'it' wants to move, all the other houses in 'its' area are up in price as well. And—''

''Enough of this 'it' pronoun,'' Cathy protested. '' 'It' really doesn't apply to anyone except Tom.''

"True," James Murray said with a smile, then added, "So, what if the homeowner wants to sell, and then rent? Then the rise in value has helped him."

"Yes, admittedly then it has. But you know something funny? That seldom happens. Aging adults who voluntarily sell and then move to an apartment or old-folks' home are few and far between. In most instances, people die still owning their homes. So, in a way, they haven't benefited from their homes' increased value. As Tom mentioned earlier, our government not only promotes home ownership, but also, through its 'rollover rule,' promotes perpetual home ownership. Late in their lives, after years of escalating house values, few people want to sell their houses and incur capital-gains tax—especially because by then their principal residences are no longer houses, they're homes!"

Roy's argument was valid. Of Sue's and my eight grandparents, six had died homeowners. And even though my surviving grandmother, the devoted Lions fan, now lives at Heaven's Gate, she still owns her old home.

"What your house is worth, frankly, is of no financial significance whatsoever if you have no intention of ever selling it. That's why many financial experts have noted that home ownership should, in most cases, be part of a financial plan but it shouldn't be the entire financial plan. On its own, such a plan can't survive. You can't spend your house! Even if you do plan on selling your house later in life and renting or buying a lower-cost accommodation, you certainly don't want to be forced to do so in case you change your mind later. Home ownership must work in conjunction with saving ten percent, building a retirement fund, and being properly insured. Heck, the people I've known, friends of my mother's who have sold their houses and moved to retirement homes, did so at such an advanced age that they couldn't fully enjoy the proceeds of the sale anyway."

"We're not in total agreement here, Roy." This was no surprise, coming from James Murray. "I've known several people who have sold their homes and used the proceeds to augment their retirement income. In addition, the people who haven't sold live rent-free now."

"Agreed," Roy acknowledged, "but I would argue that the real costs of home ownership, even without a mortgage, come close to the cost of renting an adequate apartment. Property tax, insurance, utilities, upkeep, and let us not forget time, add up to a hefty annual cost—an often underestimated hefty annual cost.

"I don't want to belabor this point. I do think home ownership is an excellent investment—one of the best. But excellent and perfect are not synonymous. I just want to inform our young friends here, especially the single ones, that renting is not throwing your money away. Look at Clyde, that slothful soul. He's rented all his life, and because his monthly costs to rent have been substantially less than his costs would have been to own, he's been able to spend more on other things, and he's been able to save more than ten percent of his income."

"Even though I do believe in real estate, I'm happy to hear you say all this, Roy," Tom admitted. "The investment merits of home ownership appeal to me, but I hate fixing things, cutting the lawn, wallpapering, and all that domestic junk. And I don't really need the space. Plus, if I bought even a small house on my salary, I'd definitely feel the pinch. I could do it, but I wouldn't have much money left over for traveling and golfing . . . and girls."

"Yeah, your fantasy life is pretty rich," Cathy teased.

"There you go," Roy said to James Murray triumphantly. "A perfect example of someone who is better off renting. Don't worry, though, James. Now he'll have more money to buy bargain properties with his brother, so you'll still make money from him."

"It may interest you to know, Roy, that with half of my commission from Tom's deal, I had their driveway repaved," James Murray bristled.

"It's true, Roy," Tom verified. "I don't mean to blow his cover, but James Murray is a generous guy."

"Boy, James, I bought my condo from you, and you didn't even take me out for lunch," Cathy complained, with a wink.

"Speaking of your condo, Cathy, there's an example of a sound investment decision." Roy's compliment seemed to surprise my sister. "With your income, and your expensive tastes, I'm sure you wanted a nice place overlooking the marina. Am I right?"

"Yes," Cathy replied sheepishly.

"Well, there's a perfect example of a case where it was better to buy. I'm sure your mortgage costs and condo fees are about the same as the rental costs for a comparable location."

"Almost exactly the same. That's why I decided to buy." Cathy shrugged. "I figured I might as well be an owner if the costs weren't any different."

"Well, they were a little different in that, by buying, you gave up the use of your down payment. But, nonetheless, you did make the right move. Plus, you bought a condo, so you won't have to be involved in maintenance and repairs."

"I just don't have time for that, Roy," Cathy agreed.

"Dave, you seem to be heading in the right direction, too. With a child on the way and Sue working out of the home, you'll need the space a house provides. That fact, combined with the investment and tax merits of home ownership, leads me to conclude that buying a house is probably the right move for you," Roy stated, as he brushed off my shirt.

"'Probably' is not the word I want to hear, Roy." I frowned as I abdicated the barber chair to Tom.

"I say 'probably' because there is one time when even the individual to whom home ownership seems ideally suited is best not to buy."

"Now there's a contradictory sentence," I noted.

"No, Dave, that situation can exist. Just ask the folks in Dallas. If house prices are about to drop, obviously one is best not to buy," Roy responded.

136

"Yeah, obviously," I consented. "But Dallas was different. It was basically a one-industry town. When oil went down, so did the town. Ann Arbor, on the other hand, is a more diversified community. Certainly, in areas not dominated by one industry we don't have to worry about real estate ever declining."

"You're wrong. Real estate can go down. In most areas, real estate has been on a steady climb since the depression, but no trend lasts forever. Need I mention New England?" Roy cautioned.

"Roy, I respect your opinion, and I realize you know a tremendous amount about financial matters, but nobody I read thinks real estate is going to go down," Cathy argued. "They're not making any more land."

"The famous *finite-land* argument," Roy laughed. "Yes, there is a finite amount of land, albeit that it works out to scores of acres per capita in the U.S.

"Look, I'm not saying real estate is definitely going to go down. But I do want to alert you to that possibility.

"Over the last several years, a few factors have combined to cause the prices of houses in many areas to skyrocket. Women have entered the work force in unprecedented numbers. Americans are having fewer children than they did generations ago. Both of these developments result in higher disposable family incomes. Much of that higher disposable income is being spent on housing. In addition, the baby-boom generation has matured and is fueling an increase in the demand for housing. And, on top of all that, people are no longer averse to borrowing heavily. In fact, over the past fifty years borrowing has gone from a shameful vice to the national pastime. Instant gratification is our society's modus operandi. The consumer-debt rate is alarming."

"Roy, you should be writing doom and gloom books, not cutting hair," lamented James Murray. "As long as people can service the debt, what's the problem?"

"As long as they can service the debt, there is no problem. But two things can happen that can lead to an inability to carry that debt. One: rising interest rates. Everyone—consumers, corporations, and, most of all, governments—is in debt up to the eyeballs. Unless North America enjoys uninterrupted growth, that mountain of debt will someday lead to higher interest rates—not permanently higher rates, perhaps, but higher rates nevertheless. Think about it. If everyone needs money, doesn't it follow that the cost of money will eventually go up? If everyone wants licorice, you can bet it will rise in price. Money is no different. So far—''

''The debt problem isn't new, Roy. Why haven't rates shot way up in the last few years?'' Tom probed.

''Because, up until recently, we have enjoyed excellent economic growth. Growth that has enabled most to service their debts and still enjoy a higher standard of living. But, during these years of growth, the debt has also continued to grow. And each year of sustained growth brings us one year closer to an inevitable slowdown. We've always had recessions . . . and we always will.

''The slowdown will lead us to the second thing that can make carrying debt difficult. Economic woes: layoffs, shutdowns, lower incomes, et cetera, et cetera. In these days of one-hundred-and-fifty-thousand-dollar mortgages, our society can't afford too many layoffs. All of you remember 1980 and '81. You remember how a recession works. Harold, the car salesman, sees his income drop from sixty thousand to twenty-nine thousand. He can no longer afford his fifteen-hundred-dollar-a-month mortgage payment, so he has to sell. But—uh-oh! Where are the buyers? Nobody else is doing too well, either. Harold drops his asking price daily, until he finally sells his house for thirty thousand less than he paid for it.''

''Whoa, now, Roy. That may have happened in some areas, but it certainly wasn't the norm. In most diversified communities, real-estate prices held their own!'' James Murray exclaimed.

''That's true. But at the time of that recession, debt levels weren't as high. And working women, smaller families, and the maturing baby-boom generation were not totally factored into the prices of homes. I believe they are now. James, the bottom line is that, in certain parts of this country, the prices of houses have risen to the point where they bear little relation to the houses' true value. If I were buying today, I would be careful," Roy recommended, somewhat ominously.

"Roy, why the hell didn't you tell me this before I closed my deal?" Tom demanded intensely.

"For a number of reasons, Tom. One: As Cathy pointed out, not all experts share my somewhat pessimistic view. Two: I don't think real estate is going to collapse. I do believe, however, that it may, in several areas, have some down years. It's still a fine, fine long-term investment. Three: You bought an undervalued property in an area that has not been subject to the tremendous run-up in prices. Four: You bought near water. I know that sounds funny, but it's a fact of real-estate investing that property near water seldom loses its value. Five: Your brother is capable of increasing the value of the place handsomely with little expense. Last: You fixed your mortgage costs, and your rental income is certain for three years. All in all, I think you're in fine shape even if we do see tough times.

"The people who I think should be worried, or at least careful, are the ones who have a lot of heavily leveraged property without a lot of other assets backing them up."

"What about me, Roy? Would you suggest I wait to buy?" I asked eagerly.

"No, Dave. As I said earlier, with the baby about to arrive and Sue working at home, it would be nice for you to own a home. You're in a prosperous city. You don't have to worry about losing your job. And, most important, you're a long-term investor. Besides—"

"Roy could be dead wrong," James Murray interrupted. "After all, he has been giving this sermon for years and, in most areas, real estate has continued to climb each year."

"True," Roy said with a grin, "but lately, in a growing number of regions, my preachings of caution have proved warranted.

"This is how I feel about home ownership," he continued, after reflecting for a moment. "For most people, it's an excellent investment. Leveragibility, tax incentives, forced savings, pride in ownership, and reading the paper by the fireplace make it pretty tough to beat. My house is more than just a good investment. It's also my most prized possession. All I've been trying to do is warn you that it's not always best for a person to own. But I should add, before James does, that even if you bought for the wrong reasons and at the wrong time, you would probably still fare pretty well over the years."

James Murray rose and applauded.

"Can you give me some tips on buying, Roy?" I moved on. "What should I look for?"

"When you go to buy a house, you should look at it from two angles—"

"Yeah. The front and the back," cracked Clyde.

"Good one, Clyde," was Roy's caustic rejoinder. "The house should fit your needs and wants, and it should also fill the requirements of a good investment. No one can tell you what suits your needs and wants except yourself—"

"And his wife," Clyde roared.

"And his wife," Roy agreed, "but I can give you some tips with regard to the investment side of things.

"The age-old adage about buying the worst house on a nice street and fixing it up still holds. Location remains the key to buying any real estate, including a home. Proximity to schools, to public transportation, and to shopping is also important.

"You want to make sure that as other homes rise in value, yours rises proportionately, at the least. To do this, you must make sure that potential buyers will always find your house attractive. The more potential buyers who feel that way, the better. Build a deck; people love decks. You'll get back your money and more. Buy a home with a fireplace; people love fireplaces. Minor cosmetic surgery will pay for itself many times over. Strictly from an investment standpoint, I advise you against a pool. Most people don't want one. So, when you go to sell, there will be fewer potential buyers—less demand. Less demand translates into a lower selling price."

"Yeah, but I'm one of the few who does want a pool."

"Then get one. When it comes to home ownership, it's more important to fulfill your needs and wants than to make the perfect investment. You have to live there every day."

"That's it?" I fretted. "No more tips?"

"I'm an advocate of having a home inspector go through any house you're seriously considering buying, especially if it's an older house. Remember, we're talking about one of the biggest expenditures of your life, if not *the* biggest—spending a few hundred dollars to make sure all is well is very much in order.

"Dave, I can't tell you which house to buy. Our tastes are a lot different. Buy the house you and Sue like best. That is assuming, of course, you can afford it. And I do mean truly afford it. I don't mean the 'sorry-Tom-I-can't-go-out-for-a-beer-'cause-our-mortgage-payment-is-so-big' kind of affording it. Stretching yourself to your financial limit in order to buy a house is almost always a financial mistake. It precludes your putting into practice other important financial planning strategies such as saving ten percent. It drains you of all your fun money and it's very stressful. Live within your means, even if the rest of the country isn't!"

"Should we put down as big a down payment as possible. . . or as small as possible?" I wondered.

"And what about my mortgage? Should I pay it off as quickly as possible?" Cathy added.

"First, let me respond to Dave's question. It's nice to have the option of a big down payment. Most home buyers find themselves scrambling frantically just to come up with their minimum down payment. To most of them, the thought of making a larger-than-required down payment is only a dream."

"That's true for first-time buyers, Roy, but not usually for repeat purchasers, because the equity they've built up in their homes over the years is usually greater than the required down payment on the house they're moving to," James Murray contended.

"Granted," Roy relented. "The questions of whether to make a small or large down payment and whether to pay down the mortgage as quickly as possible are really one and the same in that both are, in essence, asking the following: If you have funds available, is reducing the size of your mortgage the most attractive investment alternative?"

"No way!" Tom blurted out. "With the interest portion of each mortgage payment tax-deductible, it would be foolish to pay off the loan."

"That's right, Tom," James Murray agreed wholeheartedly. "If you're in a twenty-eight percent tax bracket and your mortgage is at eleven percent, it's only costing you around eight percent after tax because of the allowable mortgage-interest deduction. Or stated more meaningfully, you would only be earning eight percent after tax by paying it off . . . and remember, it's what you earn after tax that counts.

"That's why financial experts argue that paying down the mortgage more quickly than the lender requires doesn't make a lot of sense," James Murray concluded.

"Roy?" Cathy looked for confirmation.

"Let me start by saying that you could do a lot worse than an eight-percent-after-tax return. Especially since there are a number of other benefits to paying down the mortgage, including stress reduction, pride in ownership, and freed-up cash flow when the mortgage is eventually repaid in full.

"Those points aside, I'd agree that it may not be your best investment alternative and you'd certainly be making a mistake to sacrifice your ten percent savings, your insurance program, or your retirement planning to pay off the house faster. However, if you have surplus funds beyond what's needed for our three financial priorities, then paying down the mortgage may be worth considering. Actually, we'll talk a bit more about this subject next month, but before we leave it I should mention that I've yet to meet anyone who has paid off his mortgage early and regretted it."

"We'll talk more about this next month is right," James Murray taunted Roy, in a semi-serious fashion.

"Supposing there was a person who had a large enough discretionary cash flow to save ten percent, build a retirement fund, and pay down the mortgage, and supposing that such a person agreed with your advice, what would be the best way to implement it?"

By employing the word "suppose" liberally, Cathy was attempting not to incite Tom by reminding him of her substantially-higher-than-his income and not to annoy James Murray by siding with Roy.

"Miss Moneybags . . . must be nice!" Tom threw in immediately.

"I still think there are better alternatives," James Murray murmured.

"There are a number of possible early-paydown methods, Cathy. Some mortgages allow for prepayments of principal without penalty; some allow for biweekly payments. By paying twice a month, you end up making virtually a full additional month's payment every year. That can reduce the life of a thirty-year mortgage by almost ten years!

"Another excellent method is to shorten your amortization period. Before you ask, Dave, the amortization period is simply the length of time over which, through equal payments, a mortgage is fully paid off. Let me give you a startling example of not only how effective this strategy can be, but also how surprisingly cost-efficient it is. A seventy-five-thousand-dollar mortgage amortized over thirty years at eleven percent costs seven hundred and five dollars a month. The same seventy-five-thousand-dollar mortgage amortized over fifteen years at eleven percent would cost how much?''

Even I knew enough not to guess double the thirty-year amount.

"Eleven hundred,'' Cathy hazarded.

"Eight hundred and fifty,'' Roy announced. "Fifteen years of mortgage payments eliminated . . . fifteen years . . . for less than a hundred and fifty bucks a month.''

"And it's forced savings to boot,'' Cathy added, to Roy's obvious pleasure. "Boy, fifteen years of payments . . . that must be a savings of tens of thousands of dollars in interest . . . maybe even a hundred thousand.''

"True, Cathy, very true, but it's extremely important to remember that those interest savings had a cost—the extra one hundred and fifty a month—they weren't just created out of thin air. As James pointed out earlier, a very strong mathematical case could be made that that same one hundred and fifty a month, placed in a different investment vehicle, would have grown to be even more than the mortgage-interest savings—especially since, as we have heard many times, that interest is tax-deductible.

"That caveat aside, it's still a pretty neat example, and strong testimony to the advantage of paying down the mortgage early, if it doesn't mean sacrificing our ten percent solution, our insurance programs, or our retirement funds.

"An excellent book on this subject is *The Common-Sense Mortgage* by Peter Miller. It covers a wide variety of mortgage-related topics in a very easy-to-understand style. One of its premises is that no single mortgage format works well for all borrowers. Everyone has different needs and, what's more, constantly changing needs. Therefore, to make an informed decision you must be acquainted with a variety of possibilities—all of which are covered in this book. Read it!

"I do want to offer an opinion about the type of mortgage you should select, though. Nobody, and I mean nobody, can accurately predict the future course of short-term and long-term interest rates. There are people who are paid hundreds of thousands of dollars a year to consistently forecast interest rates incorrectly. Just think what they'd be making if they were consistently right! Because no one can predict the future with certainty, it is difficult to decide between a fixed-rate mortgage and an adjustable-rate mortgage, which fluctuates along with prevailing interest rates. 'What if I take an adjustable-rate mortgage and rates rise to eighteen percent? I'll be in big trouble.' 'What if I take a fixed-rate mortgage and rates fall three points? I will have wasted all that money.' It's a tough call.

"But James and I do agree on this point: For the majority of us, a fixed-rate mortgage is the way to go. If you know you can afford to make the payments, you should never be in trouble. Basically, you're fixing your costs and, in most cases, you can be sure your income will be rising. Sure, sometimes rates will go down and you'll regret your decision. Even then, though, you can often refinance. Yes, there are associated penalties, but if rates fall by two percent or more it's often a good move. And remember, sometimes rates will go up and you'll be thankful that you're protected. It comes down to risk versus reward. The risk is that rates may fall, and you'll be paying more than your buddies . . . but you will be surviving! The reward is that, if rates rise dramatically, you'll not be forced to sell your house. You'll have peace of mind—and that's worth a lot."

"What if rates are already at eighteen percent when you go to get your mortgage?"

"In that case, I would take an adjustable-rate mortgage, hoping rates would go down," Roy answered thoughtfully.

"But you said it's impossible to predict rates."

"I also said 'hoping,' not 'predicting.' If rates stay at that level for any significant period of time, you'll have bigger problems to worry about than your mortgage . . . like the guys with the guns on your front lawn. Certainly, the level of interest rates at the time you select your mortgage will play a part in your decision but, most of the time, I'd advise selecting fixed-rate.

"By the way, a number of experts disagree with my opinion on this matter, so you decide for yourself."

"I agree with Roy," confirmed James Murray. "There's something about locking in costs that I find attractive."

"Any questions?" Roy asked as he brushed off Tom.

"I have one. Suppose your job demands that you move every couple of years. Is home ownership still a good idea?"

"Good question, Dave. It has absolutely nothing to do with anyone in this room, but it's a good question nonetheless," Roy acknowledged with a grin. "Even the staunchest of real-estate supporters would agree that, over a one- or two-year term, it's impossible to predict price movements. They would also agree that the costs of moving—closing costs, legal fees, commissions, time, et cetera—would tend to negate any gain in value even if there was one. And if there wasn't one—well, obviously, home ownership would have been a bad move. Also, if you're moving frequently, you're a house owner, not a homeowner. It takes time to make a place your own—"

"This is a longer ans—" Tom attempted to interrupt.

"In conclusion, I would say that if you know you are going to be moving within a brief period, buying a home is a debatable move unless your employer will indemnify you against financial loss caused by either a drop in property value or the aforementioned costs."

"The one thing you didn't talk about today, Roy, is the thing that our friends complain about the most—how do you come up with the down payment? Even if I did want to buy a home, it would take me years to come up with a twenty percent down payment," Tom admitted.

"Traditionally, as you three well know, lending institutions want a twenty percent down payment, meaning that before standard financing can be arranged, you have to save tens of thousands of dollars. That's not easy. It may not be impossible, but it's not easy. If your friends are finding that it's taking too long and if they desperately want to buy a house now, there are some avenues worth considering.

"It is almost becoming the norm for young, first-time buyers to borrow money from their parents or other family members. If that's not possible, perhaps an FHA mortgage is worth looking at. They require a lot of paperwork, and not everyone qualifies for them, but for those who do, the down payment is usually only five percent. Qualified veterans can apply for a VA mortgage—often a great deal, sometimes involving no down payment.

"Foreclosures offer another possibility. Usually the seller of a foreclosure or distressed property is eager enough to get rid of the place that he or she will accept a smaller down payment.

"Borrowing part of the money from the real-estate agent is another idea. Clearly, the agent has a vested interest in closing the deal, and therefore he or she may be willing to lend the buyer a portion of the needed down payment, subject to provisions, of course.

"Even if the real-estate agent is unwilling to extend a loan, which is understandable, by the way, he or she may be able to direct you to available financing.

"It's not easy for young couples to buy a house these days. Yet, somehow, most of them manage to do it and get by just fine. I don't think this problem is new; I think it's just getting more press now because young people today think that, when they leave their parents' nest, by some divine right they should move directly into an air-conditioned birdhouse. Ah, if only life were that easy!"

"I hate to admit it, Roy, but you're right about me and my contemporaries. We do tend to have high, and often unrealistic, expectations. Fortunately, some of us are doing our best to learn how to not only meet those expectations, but to surpass them . . . with your help, of course," I thanked him indirectly.

"Next month?" Tom prompted.

"Saving, spending, and credit management."

"Gee, Cathy could be a guest expert on one of those three," Tom tossed over his shoulder as we left the shop.

Chapter 8

Saving Savvy

I ENTERED ROY'S TO A standing ovation.

"Here he is! The father of the year!" Roy beamed with pride.

"Samantha?" James Murray tsk'ed, while a painfully tone-deaf Clyde hummed the *Bewitched* theme song. "Were you an Elizabeth Montgomery fan when you were young?"

"You think you're kidding. That's exactly why we chose Samantha," I answered honestly. "Both Sue and I loved that show."

"Hey, guys, I'm expecting my nephew to be named either Darrin or Dr. Bombay," Cathy tossed in. "And does this mean that I have to marry a man named Arthur?"

"Clyde, what's with the black armband?" Tom wondered.

"I'm wearing it out of respect for you, Dave, James, and Roy . . . and out of respect for your dear departed Tigers, the once-proud ball club . . . a sad moment indeed," Clyde sympathized, with all the sincerity of a game-show host.

"We'll get 'em next year." My rebuttal was woefully short of conviction.

"Back to a more cheerful topic, Dave," Roy rescued me from despair. "How are Sue and the baby? Everything went well?"

"Perfectly. Sue was only in labor for three hours. I myself played a major part in the delivery. I told her, 'Breathe in, breathe out'—"

"Good advice," Clyde interjected sarcastically.

"To answer your other question, Roy, they're both just great. Sam is beautiful. She takes after her mother, thank goodness," I added before one of them could.

"Can she wiggle her nose?" wondered Jimmy.

"Everyone's a comedian," I noted.

"And word has it that you bought a house, too. Congratulations!"

"Thanks, Roy. Yeah, it's been quite a month. We bought an older home on a nice quiet street in Ann Arbor. Hard as it may be to believe, we actually spent around ten thousand dollars less than we had planned to. We took one look at the place and knew it was the house for us. The previous owners had really kept it up well. It has a new roof and a new furnace. The pipes and the wiring were just redone seven years ago. We have a den, a sunroom, and even a gazebo. You guys should come and see it . . . No, come to think of it, we're busy that weekend."

"All right, let's get started," Roy broke in. "I'm in a real hurry. I have to close up shop by ten-thirty. Marj's niece, Laura, is getting married in Flint. Yowza," he yawned. "Yep. I'm pretty excited about the whole thing."

"C'mon, Roy. Give and take. I'm sure Marj isn't always thrilled about everything she has to do with you," countered Cathy.

"In my defense, Cathy, I didn't complain at all when I had to go to Laura's first two weddings. But now that her *sacred* day has become an annual event, Marj's and my nerves are wearing thin . . . as is our pocketbook." This comment drew a laugh from everyone.

"I've got to warn you, Roy," Tom began. "I was saying on the way here that, for the first time in half a year,

I wasn't particularly looking forward to our monthly trip to the barber. Your guidance on how to create wealth has been fantastic, but it's hard to get psyched up about a lecture on the merits of thrift. Don't buy fancy cars; don't abuse credit cards; don't borrow to go on trips; look after the nickels and dimes, and the dollars will look after themselves; don't underestimate the power of coupons; a penny sa—"

"We get the point," Roy put an abrupt end to the litany. "But my philosophy on today's subject might surprise you."

"What exactly is today's subject? Tom seems to think he knows. But all you said last month was that we were going to discuss saving, spending, and credit management. So," I ventured, "is what we're really talking about the proper handling of our day-to-day financial affairs?"

"That's not a bad way of putting it," Roy commended me. "In this instance, by 'saving,' I mean saving for things like trips, VCRs, and cars, not saving as in the ten percent fund and retirement funds. By 'spending,' I mean purchasing goods from groceries to large-screen TVs, not investing. And by 'credit management,' I mean the use of credit cards, lines of credit, and personal loans, not investment loans and mortgages. So, the proper handling of our day-to-day financial affairs is probably a perfect description of today's agenda."

"But Tom probably wasn't far off the mark with his little routine, either," Cathy speculated. "You are going to give us a lecture on the merits of thrift, comparison shopping, and a debt-free net-worth statement."

"I confess that I used to espouse, in fact 'preach' may be a better word, the benefits of those things. Historically, my lesson on today's subject wasn't unlike Tom's speech at all."

Tom asked the obvious question, "What happened to change that?"

"Nobody listened." Roy's wry chuckle didn't mask the seriousness of his response. "Oh, I shouldn't say nobody.

Some of my pupils followed my advice on saving, spending, and credit management. Well, at least one did. And he's certainly not in this room." Roy nodded toward James Murray, Jimmy, and Clyde.

"After all—" Tom started.

"Let me finish," Roy said politely. "Almost everyone I've taught over the years has developed the winning habit of saving ten percent of his or her income and investing it for growth. I would guess that ninety-five percent of them have drafted wills, and purchased and maintained appropriate life insurance. And, of course, they've contributed to the retirement plans of their choice. Basically, they've combined common sense with simple but effective strategies to move toward all of their financial goals.

"But when it came to following my advice about day-to-day things like developing household budgets, avoiding credit cards, and exercising a degree of self-control—which is really all thrift is—generally, people ignored me."

"Why?" Cathy huffed. "If it weren't for you, many of those people would have faced bleak financial futures."

"As one who chose to ignore the teachings of a man whom he once called 'his financial savior,' perhaps James could answer that question."

We all turned our attention to James Murray. He smiled. "Saving ten percent of your income and investing it in a properly selected long-term growth vehicle; making a will; buying the proper amount and type of life insurance; building a retirement fund—these have three great features in common. First, they are easy to understand. You don't have to be a mathematical genius to grasp the advantages of something like dollar cost averaging. Second, they work. All of your financial goals can be achieved through the application of these principles. What's more, they can be achieved without a significant lowering of your current standard of living. Third, and equally important, the guidelines are easy to implement and easy to maintain.

"So, I was moving toward the attainment of all my financial goals, and I didn't have to study the stock-market pages for hours a week. I didn't have to phone my broker four times a day. I didn't have to spend every Saturday afternoon reading books on investing. While my net worth continued to grow, I played tennis.

"Then Roy sat me down and explained why I should develop a household budget. He told me to keep track of every dime I spent, to read the newspapers each night and write down the items on special, and to save—never borrow—money to go on a trip. I remember him saying, 'You'll enjoy your vacation more, knowing it's paid for.'

"Even as Roy spoke, I knew there was no way that I was going to follow any of that advice. Drive across town to get chicken on special? Get serious! Develop a budget and keep track of every cent? That's just not my style. Ease of implementation? Uh-uh!"

"Let me take it from here, James," Roy commanded. "A couple of years after I had taught James the basics of sound financial planning, we got together to review his progress. His report card read straight A's. His net-worth statement was impressive, and getting more so each day. I commended him, and myself, on a job well done. So, imagine my surprise when he admitted that he had not followed any of my advice on the managing of day-to-day financial matters! Then he told me that practically no one else had, either."

Cathy frowned in consternation. "Were you upset?"

"No, not at all. I quickly realized that, if anything, I should feel a deep sense of satisfaction. My overall financial plan had worked in spite of its users' undisciplined approach to daily saving, spending, and credit management. Then I realized that it's really no concern of mine how someone manages his or her day-to-day finances. People weren't coming to me to be told that they shouldn't eat out more than once a week. They were coming to me to learn how they could eventually afford to eat out every night if they wanted to."

"The fact is," Clyde asserted, "what the hell does it matter how I spend my money if I'm already takin' care of my financial planning?"

"Once again, Clyde, you have articulated my point perfectly." Roy chuckled. "I hate to admit it, but Mr. Eloquence here is right. Our ten percent savings, retirement plan contributions, insurance premiums, and mortgage payments or rent are coming off the top, that is, not being taken from whatever is left over at the end of the month. So, how we spend our discretionary income has astonishingly little impact on our financial future. As long as people are following the rest of our financial planning guidelines, how they handle day-to-day finances can safely be left up to them."

"I've got a question, Roy," I declared. "In April or May you spoke out against budgeting. Now you're saying that, in the past, you've advocated it. Why?"

"The type of budgeting I touched on in the spring is distinctly different from the budgeting I used to recommend to people like James. Nine times out of ten, budgeting that is done to create a savings fund for the future is a losing proposition. As I pointed out months ago, it's virtually impossible to budget accurately for both needs and wants. Too often, through rationalization, the wants become needs and the seemingly well-balanced budget goes out the window. The type of budgeting that I was recommending to James and others was a household monthly expense budget—a budget confined strictly to needs. To be honest, I still feel that type of budget can be very useful. It's comparable to the shop budget that has worked so well for me over the years," Roy explained.

"You see," James Murray took over, "most people, including most financial planners, have it backwards. They develop intricate budgets that cover everything from weekly gas expenses and entertainment costs to saving for retirement. Unfortunately, because most of us lack self-discipline, today's concerns receive the bulk of our financial resources. The hundreds of dollars that were supposed

154

to be there at the end of the month to buy a mutual fund and to start up a retirement fund have shrunk or vanished. 'The damn budget's not working,' people cry. But, by following Roy's advice, we are taking care of financial planning first. We can be capricious with the rest of the money, or we can set aside so much for a trip, so much for a new car, so much for groceries—you know, save the way abnormal people like Roy do. It's really a matter of style. But, because you are paying yourself first and using forced-saving techniques, someday you'll be wealthy no matter how you manage your day-to-day finances.

"If a financial planner looked at the way Jimmy, Clyde, and I handle our daily finances, he would probably have a heart attack. We buy groceries at variety stores. We get our gas at full-service stations. We don't pay our credit cards off every month. We join health clubs and don't go. Our day-to-day money management is an embarrassment. But we sure look pretty in *the big picture*. In fact, our net-worth statements look great. None of us will ever have any real financial worries," James Murray concluded.

I was skeptical. "You don't condone this behavior, do you, Roy?"

"Of course not. Using some discipline and common sense, you can get a lot more out of your money than these guys do. But I have to agree that, despite their devil-may-care approach to saving, spending, and credit management, all three of them are in excellent financial shape," Roy acknowledged.

"The problem is that I'm not going to have enough money left after all this forced saving to enjoy myself. I'm going to have to become a miser and a bookkeeper who budgets as meticulously as you," I worried.

"Not true, Dave," was Roy's straightforward response. "Not true at all. I realize that implementing the strategies that we've discussed sounds like a lot, but it's really not that bad. You've all agreed that setting aside ten percent of your net income, especially when using forced-saving techniques, is relatively painless. In fact, I'll bet you don't even notice the sacrifice."

"Agreed," I conceded.

"Your insurance costs are not overly burdensome. And even though your saving for retirement involves some sacrifices, they're hardly crippling. Remember, as I said a few months ago, you have to do some saving and planning for your future—you're going to spend the rest of your life there. Certainly, the plan I've laid out for you isn't too much to ask of yourselves."

"Just think, Dave." An animated James Murray leapt to his feet. "Without doing anything fancy or risky, and without pinching your standard of living very much, you and Sue are on your way to accomplishing all of your financial goals. And all the while, as you sleep like a baby, your friends are tossing and turning, wondering and worrying about their finances."

"What if Dave goes out and buys a large-screen TV with a built-in stereo? Or what if Sue becomes a charge-aholic and runs up thousands of dollars on the credit card?" Cathy demanded. "I know that their financial planning is assured through forced savings. But I don't think that means they can do and buy whatever they want."

"Of course it doesn't, Cathy," Roy agreed. "I would consider that to be 'gross mishandling of discretionary income'—a common malady in this country. I would rank that right up there with the couple that earns an annual income of forty thousand dollars, and buys a brand-new, thirteen-thousand-dollar car with no money down. What they've managed to do is drain their monthly cash flow, use borrowed money to buy a non-durable good, and lose thousands of dollars as soon as their *investment* is driven off the lot. From a financial planning standpoint, that is not smart. Neither, however, is it fatal. Most people, even those I've taught, buy new cars with borrowed money all the time. It may not be smart—but I guess it's fun and, for most, affordable.

"Now, the couple that earns an annual income of forty thousand dollars and buys a brand-new, twenty-five-thousand-dollar car with no money down is just plain foolish. Several people in their twenties and thirties have come to me for financial planning advice. I can't believe the number of young people who want not only to achieve all the goals we've discussed, but also to own a beautiful house, a fancy car, and a vacation property . . . now! They don't need a financial planner; they need a miracle worker! People must live within their means. That doesn't mean they have to scrimp and save every day of their lives, but it does mean they can't spend with reckless abandon. People who do live within their means not only are easily able to implement our financial planning strategies, but also they lead a much less stressful life.

"Charles Dickens's Mr. Micawber put it best: 'Annual income twenty pounds, annual expenditure nineteen nineteen-six, result happiness. Annual income twenty pounds, annual expenditure twenty pounds ought and six, result misery.'"

Truer words were never spoken.

"I have two more questions, Roy," I admitted apologetically. "One of the goals we spoke of earlier hasn't been covered: the ability to finance our children's college education."

"We'll discuss that in November, in our *miscellaneous* lesson," Roy promised. "You know—November, the month you three are going to present me with a modest token of your appreciation for all that I've done for you."

"What can we get a man who has everything?" Tom asked half-seriously.

"Good point, Tom. Let's see. I've never been given a tip," Roy joked.

"Speaking of tips, you mentioned that you used to give them on the management of day-to-day finances. Can you pass along a few to those of us who do want to make the most of our discretionary money? As everyone knows, it's a job requirement in the teaching profession that you be thrifty—"

"Cheap," Tom corrected me.

"I thought it was also mandatory that, as a teacher, you marry a teacher. How did you get around that one?" Jimmy snickered.

"I'd be happy to give you some tips." Roy's readiness surprised me, considering his time constraints and his earlier claim that he no longer concerned himself with his pupils' handling of day-to-day money. "It's nice to hear from a person who understands the value of a hard-earned dollar." Roy paused to look smugly at James Murray before returning his attention to me. "I won't design a budget for you or teach you how to haggle, one of my specialties, but I will pass on a few rules of thumb.

"First, a dollar saved is two dollars earned." Roy didn't just say this. He pronounced it. The shop fell silent.

"Think about the significance of that," he encouraged us, breaking the spell.

"I don't even understand it." Cathy spoke hurriedly, aware of the time. "What do you mean, 'A dollar saved is two dollars earned'?"

"Dave, if you got a two-dollar bonus at work, how much more would you take home?"

"It was Cathy who didn't understand, Roy, not me," I refreshed his memory. "I'd take home a little more than a dollar. By the time all my deductions had come off, almost half my bonus would be gone. Income taxes, Social Security, retirement plan contributions . . . they all add up."

"They sure do," Roy agreed. "A two-dollar raise often translates into only a one-dollar increase in disposable income . . . the same increase that would result from saving a single dollar.

"If, by buying at a liquidation sale, Tom saves two hundred dollars on the price of a VCR, it amounts to pretty much the same thing as getting a four-hundred-dollar bonus. Many people would work overtime on a holiday weekend to earn a four-hundred-dollar bonus, but those same people can't be bothered to spend three hours comparison shopping. It doesn't make sense! To be called cheap is an insult—it implies a mean and petty approach to money. What some people don't realize is that to be called thrifty is a compliment—it implies a disciplined, economical, and common-sense approach to money. It certainly was a virtue during the depression, when I was young! Food for thought, isn't it?"

Even James Murray, Jimmy, and Clyde, the resident spendthrifts, clearly appreciated Roy's point.

"Credit cards are antithetical to well-managed finances," was Roy's second pronouncement. "We all know that if we don't pay off our debt the month it is incurred, it's subject to exorbitant rates of interest. The rate on credit-card debt is often five or six percentage points higher than on standard consumer loans—so don't carry any! If you can't pay off your balance, borrow from the bank, pay off the credit-card company, and owe the bank the money. Their interest rate will be much lower."

"As long as you pay your cards off promptly, they're a pretty good deal, though, right? One month interest-free plus the convenience." Credit-Card Cathy desperately wanted Roy's approval.

She was in for a disappointment. "Actually, no. For most people, they're not a good deal. The convenience that you view as an attribute can combine with human nature to form a destructive force, especially in the hands of someone who loves to shop. How many times have you bought something with your credit card that you wouldn't have bought if you'd had to pay cash? And isn't it usually something that you know you could live without? Then how many times have you opened your credit-card bill, clutched your throat, and shrieked, 'Five hundred dollars! What the heck did I spend it on?' So, the fact is that many people who pay off their balance each month are still hurt by their use of credit cards."

"That's me." Tom shook his head ruefully. "I never paid one red cent in interest to a credit-card company, but I still cut up my cards last year. Plainly stated, I was abusing the privilege."

"I have to give you credit, Tom—no pun intended," Cathy sighed. "I should do the same . . . but I don't want to hurt the American economy." I wasn't sure Sis was kidding.

"Many people 'abuse the privilege,' as our friend here so aptly put it. At least you know yourself well enough to admit it, Tom. Credit cards do offer short-term, interest-free financing, and convenience, but they are not for the undisciplined," Roy summarized.

"Shouldn't we try to avoid consumer debt altogether, not just credit-card debt?"

"Theoretically, yes. I say 'theoretically' because, in some cases, taking on consumer debt can work to the borrower's advantage. But I'll get back to that in a minute.

"If you see a compact-disc player that you simply have to have, what's the best way to save for it?" the wealthy barber continued.

"By paying yourself first," Cathy ventured.

"Yeah, by using forced savings," Tom concurred. "It doesn't really matter whether you're saving for retirement or saving for a compact-disc player. The most effective way to do it is by paying yourself first."

"Absolutely correct! So, if Dave, for example, wants that player, he should arrange to have so much a month come directly off his paycheck and go into his account. When he has accumulated enough, he will withdraw the funds and buy the CD player. Tom hit the nail on the head when he said that it doesn't matter whether you're saving for retirement or for a luxury item—pay yourself first! The only difference is how you invest the savings. It doesn't take long to save for a consumer item or a trip. For that reason, you must invest the savings conservatively. Equity mutual funds, real estate, and stocks are not appropriate vehicles for these savings. They offer too uncertain a short-term return. The money should be placed in a competitive, guaranteed investment.

"What I mean by 'competitive' is probably best illustrated by an example. Let's say Cathy is saving up for a car that costs twenty-three thousand dollars. After one year, she's saved ten thousand dollars—not an impossible feat on her enviable income. She's confident that she'll be able to save a thousand a month in the second year. How should she invest the ten thousand she's already accumulated? Well, she knows she's not going to need it for a year, so instead of settling for the low rates that savings accounts pay, she should buy a one-year CD. She should purchase the CD from an institution that is covered by the Federal Deposit Insurance Corporation and that offers a good rate. Don't settle for whatever rate your own bank is offering—shop the market. What I'm really saying is that investing this type of savings should be governed by one thing: common sense."

"Earlier, you said that taking on consumer debt can sometimes work to the borrower's advantage," Tom recalled. "When is that true?"

"Can any of you tell me?" Roy challenged us.

"I can!" Cathy had waited a long time to vindicate her passion for plastic. "Debt is the ultimate forced-saving plan. You have to make your payments or . . . or—"

"Or you're in big trouble," Tom helped out.

"Precisely," Roy smiled. " 'The ultimate forced-saving plan' is an excellent way to phrase it, Cathy. There's no way a spendthrift like James would ever have saved up enough money to buy that beautiful RV of his—he doesn't have the discipline. By borrowing, he forced himself to save . . . after purchase, mind you, but still he had to save. And he could enjoy his acquisition in the meantime." For once, James Murray chose not to disagree or expand upon a point.

"I'm not suggesting that every time you want something you go out and borrow the money you need to buy it . . . Cathy," Roy said pointedly. "Sooner or later,

161

you would end up in bankruptcy court. And, not only can excessive borrowing tap your cash flow, it can also cause stress. You'll find sleep comes more easily when you're earning interest than when you're paying it.

"Another thing that bothers me about *borrow-to-buy* is that you miss out on the feeling of satisfaction that comes from saving up to buy something you really want. Today, some young adults have never experienced that feeling of deferred gratification. They have borrowed to buy literally every major asset they have—from their TVs and their cars to their homes."

"There's a lot of truth in what you're saying, Roy," I chimed in. "Sue and I saved for three years to buy our car outright, and it gave us a tremendous feeling. I honestly think that we enjoy the car more because we know it's fully ours."

"Sure. Because, while borrowing does have the advantage of forcing you to save, it also has the disadvantages we named earlier. Live within your means!" Roy cautioned us again, while trimming Tom's bangs at a record clip.

"I have one question, Roy, and once you've answered it, I promise I'll get these two guys out of your hair."

"It's a deal, Cathy."

"Why did you used to recommend to people that they keep track of every dime they spent? That's a lot of work, and is there really any benefit? I mean, what can you do about money that's already gone?"

"The reason I advocated, and still advocate, keeping a detailed *household financial summary* is that it can be very informative. If you don't believe me, try it. Keep a detailed summary of all of this month's expenditures.

"A couple of years after I took over the barbershop, I borrowed money to buy a new car. When I summarized my expenses at the end of the year, I couldn't believe how much of my income was spent on my vehicle. Financing costs, gas, insurance, upkeep . . . close to a third of my after-tax income hit the road with my car. It was clear that, although I could pay all my car-associated expenses, I couldn't truly afford the car I was driving. It required too many other sacrifices. So, I sold the car and bought a good secondhand one—or a 'previously owned' one, as they like to say now."

"I've never done a 'household financial summary,' as Roy calls it, and I never will." James Murray smirked. "A friend of mine did one, though, and I have to admit he benefited from it. He went into shock when he discovered that, over a twenty-two business-day period, he had spent two hundred and fifty dollars on lunches. That could add up to three grand a year! Needless to say, he's occasionally brown-bagging it now," he laughed.

True to her word, Cathy began to usher Tom and me toward the door. "Thanks for everything, Roy," we said over our shoulders.

"I was just doing a little personal household financial summary in my mind, as you people babbled on," Tom yelled as Cathy dragged us further out of Roy's. "And do you know what I spend far too much on? Haircuts! I'm spending far too much on haircuts!"

Roy just waved.

Chapter 9

Insights into Investment and Income Tax

"COFFEE?" ROY OFFERED US, WITH a warm smile.

"Hell, I d-d-don't even d-d-drink c-coffee, but I'll have one," Tom replied, teeth chattering. Cathy and I just nodded our heads, shivering and stamping our feet.

"I can't remember a colder day for this time of year. That wind chills you right to the bone . . . you can see your breath . . . and in your case, Tom, it's not a pretty sight," James Murray quipped, to the great amusement of Clyde.

"What the heck is the temperature?" Cathy grimaced.

"Minus somethin'," Clyde stated authoritatively.

"Hey, Clyde, I didn't realize you studied meteorology at school," Tom said facetiously.

"No, I hate that metric stuff," Clyde fired back. We can only hope that he was kidding.

"Roy, before we get started with today's lesson, I want to tell you that something you said last month had a profound effect on me," Cathy announced.

"You mean it took five months for me to say something that had a profound effect on you?" Roy laughed. "I must be doing something wrong."

"That's not what I meant and you know it. Serious—"

"Let me guess what it was," Tom interrupted. "A dollar saved is two dollars earned."

"You must be psychic!"

"Not psychic—psycho," Jimmy called from the back room.

"That same statement had quite an impact on me, too," Tom explained. "I hadn't thought about it before, but Roy was definitely right. Most of us will do anything to earn a few extra bucks, but very few of us will spend even a couple of hours looking for the best deal on, say, a new set of golf clubs.

"Golf clubs come to mind for a reason. Last week, I headed out to buy a new set of irons. I knew exactly what make and model I wanted but, instead of just walking into the local pro shop and paying whatever was asked, I decided to check around. I found the same set of clubs for one hundred and eighty dollars less at a different pro shop. Shopping around for only three hours saved me almost two hundred bucks. Not bad . . . not bad at all."

"And remember," I commented, "saving one hundred and eighty dollars is the same as earning a bonus of three hundred and sixty dollars."

"Well, in my case, not quite," Tom corrected me. "For me, saving a hundred and eighty dollars is the same as earning a bonus of about three hundred. But my three-hour comparison-shopping effort still *earned* me a hundred dollars an hour. It has taken twenty-nine years, but I think I've finally learned the value of being thrifty."

"Thriftiness remains a virtue," Roy summarized.

"What's today's topic, Roy?" Cathy asked eagerly. "I seem to recall that October's lesson was to be on investing."

"Today we're going to cover two distinct areas, the first of which is, indeed, investing. Our second topic is everyone's favorite: income tax." Needless to say, this was greeted by a chorus of boos. "Whoa, my friends, do not boo! We are not just going to discuss income tax; we are going to discuss how to reduce our annual income-tax bills.'' Naturally, this remark met with a more favorable response.

"Why are we discussing investing and income tax on the same day?'' I wondered. "Do they dovetail well from a teaching standpoint?''

"The reason that we're discussing them together is quite complex, but here it is . . . '' Roy paused and looked pensive. "In terms of time, they each take approximately one haircut to cover.''

"That is deep,'' Tom deadpanned.

"I don't know much about investing, Roy, but I do know that even a teacher as skilled as you can't cover all the ins and outs of investing during one haircut—not even if the client is Rapunzel.''

"You're right, Cathy,'' Roy conceded. "To cover the ins and outs of all the different types of investments in that short a time would be impossible. But that's OK, because one of the chief prerequisites of a financial plan is that its successful implementation not be dependent on expert investment management by the *plannee*. Why? Because most of us aren't capable of performing in-depth investment analysis and, what's more, most of us don't even want to become capable!''

"Amen,'' I said fervently.

"Successful investing is elusive. If it weren't, everybody would be shopping on Rodeo Drive. Few have the time it takes to properly analyze different investment alternatives. Those who do have the time to assess the risks and rewards of a given investment must also have both strong mathematical ability and sufficient knowledge to enable them to apply that ability wisely. That might involve anything from having an accounting background when studying stocks to having a feel for the local economy when selecting a commercial real-estate site.''

"I'm sorry to interrupt you here, Roy,'' apologized James Murray. "But I want to reiterate something I said way back in May. Successful investing takes not only a lot of time and specialized knowledge, but also tremendous discipline and an eye for value—an eye that is often more intuitive than informed."

"I would go one step further, James, and say that, without discipline and an eye for value, an investor is doomed to dismal failure. I know several well-trained, well-informed investors who consistently lose money. They lack either the required discipline or the eye for value. Conversely, I know people who lack specialized knowledge but still have successful investment records because of their discipline and eye for value.

"Remember in May when James pointed out that, to make money in the stock market, you have to 'buy low, sell high'?" Roy asked us.

"It doesn't take a genius to figure that out," I replied.

"No? Then why do most market investors do the exact opposite? They buy high and sell low—a foolish approach if ever there was one."

"They lack self-discipline," Tom answered with a shrug. "Stocks are low when almost nobody wants them. So, to buy low, you have to buy at just the time when most people are saying it's not smart to do so."

"Exactly," Roy confirmed. "It may be the only law that has never been broken: the law of supply and demand. When a stock's price is low, it's down for only one reason: There are too few buyers and too many potential sellers. In other words, the stock is relatively unwanted. To buy in that kind of environment takes a courage that few of us have."

"It's the same on the sell side," I broke in. "You're supposed to sell high. When is a stock high? It's high when everyone wants it. It's high when demand is high and supply is low. It's not easy to sell a stock when all your co-workers and neighbors are telling you what a great buy it is."

"Can you see why discipline, which I define as the courage to buy when others are selling and to sell when others are buying, is so important? Without it, you're just another sheep . . . and you're probably heading toward the slaughter," Roy warned us.

"'Buy low, sell high' is impossible without self-discipline, or 'courage,' as Roy calls it," James Murray summed up.

"How about 'Buy high, sell higher'?" Tom suggested.

"Certainly it's possible but, for obvious reasons, buying low is a much less risky proposition. Many people have lost small fortunes buying late in a market rally, buying high, that is, because they convinced themselves that 'this time it will be different.' That fateful phrase has cost a lot of people a lot of money. Attempting to buy high, sell higher, is simply a fool's game," was Roy's vigorously stated philosophy.

"I would be worried about 'Buy low, sell lower,'" I admitted. "I mean, after all, aren't most stocks low just before they drop off the board?"

"True, Dave," Roy responded supportively. "Just before a gas tank hits empty, it does pass through low. That's why, along with discipline, to be a prosperous investor you must also have that eye for value. You have to recognize the difference between an investment, say a common stock, that's undervalued and one that just isn't healthy. There are many unwanted, hence low-priced, investments that are unwanted for good reason."

"What about real estate? There it seems that, for the most part, buying low and buying value aren't as important. The operative expression seems to be, 'Buy at any price, sell higher.'"

"Quite honestly, Tom, I can't put up a strong argument against your point. With the exception of some one-industry towns, real-estate prices have been on a relatively steady climb for years. Sure, during tough economic times and recessions, values have suffered, but not much. In some areas, it seems that a *bad* year is defined as a twelve-month period during which home values rise only slightly. That being said, I'd like to add the following: Most real-estate investors have enjoyed solid returns throughout the last half-century, but the ones who have exercised discipline and bought value have been even more successful. Yeah, the guy who bought an overpriced duplex toward the end of an economic boom probably did sell it for a good profit several years later. However, the canny investor who located a bargain property and bought it during a recession would have reaped even greater rewards.

"Also, and I urge you to heed my words here, in my opinion the halcyon days of guaranteed easy money in real estate are coming to an end. As I mentioned in our conversation on home ownership, no trend is permanent. There's no law that says real estate can't decrease in value. I grant you that, over the long term, well-selected real estate should always perform well. Note the term 'well-selected.' If you use discipline and common sense, and buy value, real estate will treat you well. But I don't think buying property without regard to location, timing, and value will continue to be a profitable strategy." Roy was quite adamant about this prediction.

"What worries me, Roy, is that I don't think I have the qualities you're talking about. I certainly don't have the knowledge, and I have no reason to believe I have either investing courage or an eye for value . . . especially the latter."

"Don't worry, Dave," Roy reassured me. "As I said earlier, one of the prerequisites for a sound, productive financial plan is that its successful implementation not require tremendous investment management skills on the part of the plannee."

"I remember that point vividly," I grinned. "It gave me great comfort."

"Look at your financial plan, and Cathy's," Roy continued. "You're both using professional money management, forced savings, dollar cost averaging, conservative tax-assisted retirement funds, proper insurance coverage . . . you know, all the boring things that make people wealthy. What in that plan calls for any complicated investment decisions? Before you answer, remember that

169

your short-term savings for things like cars and trips are to be invested in guaranteed products."

"I see your point, Roy, but what if, down the road, Sue and I have a lump sum to invest—say, an inheritance or royalties from a travel guide that Sue might write?"

"And what about me?" Tom cut in. "Because I'm buying real estate with my ten percent fund, I'm forced to make investment decisions. I don't have the safety net of dollar cost averaging."

"That's right, Tom, you don't," Roy answered, seemingly ignoring the fact that I had posed a question first. "I pointed out in May that when you elect to buy real estate with your ten percent fund, timing does become an issue. The discipline and eye for value we spoke of earlier are both important and, for reasons I just explained, will probably become even more so in years to come. That's the bad news. The good news is that you do seem to demonstrate those qualities. You've bought a property in an area that hadn't been subject to a tremendous run-up in prices and, what's more, you've bought a property that James described as one of the better values he had seen."

"I'm flattered that you feel that way, Roy. Unfortunately, my purchase had more to do with luck than wisdom. I didn't—"

"Yes, you did!" Roy stopped Tom abruptly. "You did recognize that property represented good value. I remember you saying that, with the size of the lot, the proximity to the water, and the nice neighborhood, the property was definitely underpriced. Don't you? James pointed out today that the eye for value is more often intuitive than informed. This is especially true of real-estate investors. Quite a few people seem to have a knack for locating potentially profitable properties. Boy, how's that for alliteration?"

"Pretty powerful," Cathy quipped.

"Another intelligent thing you did, Tom," Roy continued, "was to consult James for an opinion. His success is a testimony to his ability to spot the right property."

"Getting back to humble, little me," I tried again, "what about my lowly question? I don't have Tom's eye for value and, even if I did, I probably wouldn't use it. I don't want to be an investor; I want to be a teacher."

"Yes, even though our plans are designed to diminish, if not eliminate, the necessity for investment skills, there could possibly be times when you are faced with an investment decision. Your example of an inheritance was a good one, Dave." Roy stopped speaking long enough to get the attention of Jimmy, who was half-asleep. "Jimmy, if someone finds him or herself with excess cash from an inheritance, or from any other source, including savings from cash flow, what's the wisest investment he or she could make?"

"Pay off non-deductible debt," Jimmy shot back.

"No doubt about it," James Murray seconded.

"There is simply no better investment alternative for the average American than to pay off his or her non-deductible debt, meaning debt where the interest is not a tax-deductible expense."

"So, our mortgages are deductible debts since we can write off the interest?" I attempted to confirm my understanding.

"Right. On the other hand, what we're talking about here are debts such as car loans and credit-card balances. You are paying interest on those loans with after-tax dollars. Big deal, you say?"

We all shrugged.

"Let me put it to you this way: If, instead of paying off your twelve percent car loan, you decided to buy a certificate of deposit, what rate would the CD have to pay for that choice to result in a break-even proposition?"

Roy's question drew no immediate response.

"Eighteen percent," Cathy finally blurted out. "If I bought a CD yielding eighteen percent, because I'm in the thirty-three percent tax bracket, I would earn twelve percent after tax. That's the same value of return I am essentially *earning* by paying off a twelve percent car loan."

"Bravo! Do you two understand?"

Tom and I nodded our heads.

"Something just struck me," Tom said thoughtfully. "If paying off a twelve percent car loan equates with earning an eighteen percent interest return, just think what interest you would have to get to break even with the paying off of a credit-card debt. Some of those cards are charging as much as twenty percent on outstanding balances. You'd have to earn a thirty percent interest return just to come out even!"

"Now, I ask you, is that complex mathematics? No, of course not," Roy answered his own question. "Yet incredible numbers of Americans who have outstanding non-deductible loans also own bonds and CDs that pay fully taxable interest. It often doesn't make sense. Mr. X buys a ten-thousand-dollar CD paying around seven and a half percent. After paying tax, he's lucky if he keeps five and a half percent. At the same time, he continues to pay off his furniture loan at eleven percent with after-tax dollars. C'mon!" he scoffed.

"Knowledgeable investors agree that a three percent after-tax real rate of return is very good. Incidentally, what do I mean by 'after-tax real rate of return'?" Roy quizzed.

"The absolute rate of interest, less the amount paid in taxes, less the inflation rate," Tom expounded. "Basically, it's the amount you're gaining in purchasing power."

"Impressive. By paying off a twelve percent non-deductible loan, your after-tax rate of return is that same twelve percent, because the loan was being serviced with after-tax dollars. Let's say inflation is six percent. The after-tax real rate of return becomes, therefore, six percent —twice what is considered to be quite acceptable."

"Instead of paying off our non-deductible loans, isn't it true that we can refinance them through a home-equity loan and make them deductible?" Cathy questioned.

"Someone's been doing some reading," Tom noted enviously.

"Cathy, let's save the discussion of that strategy for our section on income taxes."

"I have a question too, Roy. Should you always pay off the highest-interest-rate non-deductible loan first?"

"Dave, it should be common sense that, if you have some money available to pay down non-deductible loans, you should pay down the one with the highest interest rate. Yet, many people put two thousand dollars down on their twelve percent car loan, and leave their eighteen percent credit-card balance untouched. Yikes! Yes, always pay off the loan with the highest associated interest rate," Roy answered diplomatically.

"There are a couple of other major considerations here," James Murray cut in. "Paying down non-deductible debt not only offers an excellent rate of return, but also is guaranteed, and there is a zero PITA factor. In addition, as Roy mentioned last month, reducing debt also reduces stress. I may not be a big fan of paying off your mortgage early—I still think there are better investment choices— but I sure agree that paying off non-deductible debt is one of the best investment alternatives."

"Well, I'm glad that it's a wise move, because it's certainly the strategy that I feel most comfortable with—no heavy analysis, zero PITA factor, and, hey, eventually it'll free up my cash flow for other things," I added.

"That's the benefit I've enjoyed the most," Jimmy reported. "Since I paid off my debts, including my mortgage . . . sorry, James . . . I've increased my ten percent fund to a fifteen percent fund, and I still have a high disposable income. In my mind, the freed-up cash flow is the most satisfying benefit of paying off debts."

"And to think we didn't even mention it, James," the wealthy barber chortled.

"What if we reach a point where we have money to invest and we have no debt?" Cathy's red face betrayed the fact that, with her lucrative income, the question was not hypothetical.

"Jimmy?" Roy redirected the question.

"Years ago, I found myself in just that position. I had accumulated several thousand dollars and I had no debt— not even a mortgage. I went to Roy and asked him for some specific investment advice. You won't believe what he told me to do. 'Spend the money!' He told me to spend it! Now, that's my type of financial planner," Jimmy concluded, giving Roy the thumbs-up sign.

"His fifteen percent fund was growing nicely, as was his retirement fund. He had no debt. He had no need for additional life insurance. His daughter's education was secure. In short, all his financial goals were being met. I suggested that he go out and buy something he'd always wanted . . . a toupee, perhaps."

Roy's advice to Jimmy didn't surprise me at all. In April, Roy had stressed that a well-designed financial plan should meet our future goals without dramatically lowering our current standard of living. In view of that, Roy's suggestion to "spend it" made perfect sense. Why shouldn't people live to the fullest once their financial futures are well taken care of?

"If you find yourself in the enviable position of having more money than you care to spend, I strongly recommend that, rather than investing it all at once, which would require a well-timed investment decision, you spread out the investment by increasing your ten percent fund monthly savings. Let's say you had an extra five thousand dollars. Put two hundred dollars more each month into your preauthorized checking plan. Obviously, the five thousand will eventually run out, and then you'll have to revert to your normal monthly saving amount. In the meantime, though, you will have invested your money wisely, taking advantage of the same strategies we've discussed before and, once again, you will have avoided having to time an investment purchase precisely."

It was hard for me to get excited about Roy's last bit of advice. Although I'm sure that I'm now on the road to prosperity, the point at which I will have more money than I care to spend is still years away.

Roy whisked me off as I stepped down from the barber chair. "On to income taxes?" I anticipated.

"I have a question first," Tom slowed us down. "Don't we ever get to buy a penny stock or something that's fun like that?"

"Mark Twain once wrote, 'There are two times in a man's life when he should not speculate: when he can't afford it, and when he can.' If you want to play the market, buy commodities, or buy options on gold, don't do it under the guise of financial planning. Yes, it can be fun. Yes, it can be exciting and, yes, on rare occasions, it can be profitable. The same things can also be said of a trip to Las Vegas. And, I should add, Las Vegas serves free drinks and is full of long-legged showgirls. Go to Vegas." Roy does have an effective way of driving a point home.

"Now on to our favorite subject: income tax.

"A dollar saved is two dollars earned," Roy repeated this familiar refrain.

"That was last month's lesson, Roy. We're covering income tax now, remember?" Tom joshed.

"A dollar saved is two dollars earned, whether it's a dollar saved through coupons or through reduced tax," James Murray mused. "What's more, a tax dollar saved is one less dollar for the government to spend, not one less dollar for you to spend."

"What James means by that is that, normally, to save a dollar we must make some sacrifice, but when we save a tax dollar, there is no associated sacrifice. Tax savings are savings of the best kind," Roy clarified. "Because of that, it's important that each of you does your best to minimize your tax bill . . . your legal best, that is. Tax evasion is illegal and is not recommended. In fact, the almost epidemic proportions that tax evasion has reached, through non-reporting of all sources of income, is one of our country's major economic woes.

"On the other hand, tax avoidance, the minimizing of one's tax bill through the proper handling of one's financial affairs, is an important part of financial planning."

"I hate to keep playing the devil's advocate," I broke in somewhat sheepishly, "but I have even less interest in becoming a tax expert than I did in becoming a knowledgeable investor. The mere mention of the word 'accounting' makes me shudder."

"Once again, your nervousness is unfounded," Roy assured me.

"We have said that one of the prerequisites of a sound and productive financial plan is that its successful implementation not be dependent on expert investment management by the plannee. Another prerequisite is that the successful implementation not be dependent upon the plannee becoming a tax expert." Tom offered an almost perfect imitation of the wealthy barber.

"You must have studied financial planning under a brilliant mentor, Tom." Roy laughed. "What Tom just said is very true. Producing and following a sound financial plan should not be dependent upon the plannee being a tax expert, not just because becoming a tax authority is an arduous task, but also because, for most of us, paying a tax consultant for his or her advice is a more cost-efficient and time-efficient approach. If your financial affairs are relatively straightforward, like those of you two boys, it won't take much time for an accountant or other tax expert to help you out. Therefore, the cost of their services will be relatively low. However, if your affairs are more complex, our captain of industry, Cathy, being a good example, then tax advice certainly will be more expensive —but obviously, more warranted, too."

"If our affairs are that simple, why don't we just do our returns ourselves?" was Tom's logical question.

"Tax reform was supposed to simplify the tax system, but it's generally agreed that it hasn't. Even a straightforward return might well benefit from a professional look-

see. As I just said, if your return is really that uncomplicated the advice won't cost much anyway."

"Remember, Tom," James Murray added, "from now
on your tax return isn't going to be as simple as Roy thinks.
You're now an owner of a rental property. Depreciation,
mortgage interest, rental income, property taxes . . . need
I say more? Even you, Dave, don't really fit in the
'straightforward' category, with Sue being self-employed.
Can you write off an office in the house? What about your
computer? Perhaps some of your car expenses are deductible?"

Tom and I looked at each other and nodded.

"You see," Roy picked up from James Murray, "there
aren't too many filers who couldn't benefit from some professional guidance."

"Well, that was a short section," Cathy kidded.
"What's on the agenda next month?"

"You don't think you're getting off that easily, do
you?" Roy replied with a wink. "I do have a few tax ideas
I'd like to pass on to you—personal favorites, if you will.
Shouldn't take more than an hour or so."

I prayed that Roy was joking.

"Two of the investments that we've already discussed
not only ease your tax burden, but also help you to achieve
a pair of extremely important financial goals, namely—"

"Retirement plans and home ownership," Tom correctly anticipated.

"Precisely," Roy confirmed. "Tax-deductibility of contributions and tax-deferred growth in the first case, and
the mortgage-interest and property-tax deductions combined with the potential deferral of capital-gains tax in
the second. Not bad . . . not bad at all . . . especially considering that, while taking advantage of all of those tax
breaks, we're accomplishing, as was just mentioned, two
very important financial planning goals. Need I say more?"

Certainly, he didn't have to say more to me because
Sue and I were, by then, not just aware of the tax

incentives but, more important, we had already begun to take advantage of them through my 403(b) plan, her Keogh, and our new home purchase. As I thought of the steps we had recently taken, I realized just how far we'd come in a few short months. Good financial planning really isn't that complex nor, fortunately, that burdensome.

"Even though I recommended that each of you seek professional tax advice, I still think it's a good idea for you to fill out your own forms," Roy interrupted my daydreaming with his apparently contradictory suggestion. "Why? Because it's an excellent learning experience. Filling out your own return is one of the best ways, if not the best, to find out what areas of your record-keeping need improvement. I would also recommend that you always complete the 1040 long form. When you use the short form you are guaranteeing yourself of paying the absolute maximum tax which can be paid on your level of income. Completing the long form will, perhaps, save you tax dollars, and definitely will familiarize you with the many available tax deductions. Even if yours don't add up to more than the standard deduction, at least the long form may point out where your tax plan needs work.

"Yes, you should still seek professional guidance, but only after you've given your return the old college try," Roy concluded.

"When you think about it, filing the long form can never result in more tax owing, only less," I remarked.

"Very good point, Dave," Roy congratulated me. "Now, I want to refer to something Cathy mentioned earlier: home-equity loans.

"Under the new tax laws, interest on consumer loans has been deemed non-deductible, which means, as we've discussed, that paying off those loans as quickly as possible is a very prudent move. Cathy suggested that instead of paying them off a person could convert them, through refinancing, to one of the still-deductible forms of debt such as a home-equity loan. It's a good point.

"Let's assume Cathy's condominium is now worth one hundred and fifty thousand dollars and the mortgage is for one hundred grand. Let's also assume she has a car loan at the bank for ten thousand dollars and owes two thousand on her credit card—"

"Only two thousand," Tom cracked.

"The interest on her car and credit-card loans would not be tax-deductible because they are consumer loans. However, if Cathy were to refinance by taking out a home-equity loan of twelve thousand, things would change dramatically. She would use the twelve thousand, of course, to pay off the other two loans."

"So, big deal," I broke in. "She still owes twelve thousand, she just owes it to a different lender."

"True," Roy replied patiently, "but the interest on the twelve-thousand-dollar loan is now tax-deductible! If the interest was fifteen hundred dollars a year, which is about right, that deduction would generate for someone in Cathy's bracket a tax savings of approximately five hundred dollars!"

"Five hundred bucks is a lot of money for making a few phone calls and filling out some forms," James Murray added. "And this was a relatively mild example. What if we're talking fifty or a hundred thousand dollars?"

"Two other points," Tom rushed in. "One: In addition to converting her non-deductible consumer loan to a deductible home-equity loan, Cathy lowered her interest expense by refinancing a credit-card debt."

Roy patted his blossoming pupil on the back.

"Two: I'm not sure that I think all of this is fair. Those who don't own homes don't have any equity to access!"

"First, don't use 'access' as a verb and second, your point is a good one. In fact, it's one more reason why home ownership is, with few exceptions, a good move— the equity that you're building gives you access to tax-efficient financing. However, it's important to note that refinancing using a home-equity loan isn't the only way of restructuring your debts to make consumer-loan interest tax-deductible. You could also take out a second mortgage—"

"Yeah, but I don't own—"

"Hold on, Tom. Or you could use the following strategy: Borrow money against the equity in your rental property and pay off your consumer loans with it. Because your rental property is an investment, the interest is tax-deductible!"

"I don't have any equity in my rental property. Remember?"

Not even Roy had an answer for that.

"I have another thought you should keep in mind," Roy continued. "Because interest on debt incurred for investment reasons is tax-deductible and consumer debt isn't, always make a concerted effort to structure your affairs so that your loans are against your investments, not your consumer goods. If that involves selling off some investments, paying off the consumer loans with the proceeds, then reborrowing to buy back the investment, so be it. In most cases, the savings will be well worth the hassle, but watch out for two things—"

"Commissions and taxes," I correctly suggested, to Roy's shock.

"Commissions and taxes," he repeated in disbelief.

"Are there any limits to how much interest we can deduct?" Cathy wondered.

"You can deduct the interest on the mortgages of your first and second homes as long as the mortgages don't exceed the price you originally paid for the homes plus the cost of any improvements. I think there's also a million-dollar cap."

"Oh, darn," I cried.

"The interest on home-equity loans may be deducted as long as the loan doesn't exceed the lesser of the fair market value of the residence less any mortgages, or one hundred thousand dollars . . . pretty generous, really.

Incidentally, a point I should have made earlier about home-equity loans is this: The undisciplined should beware! Having the ability to write a check against your home-equity line of credit is a dangerous privilege —one that's been abused by many people. Spending money frivolously and making poor investments can sometimes cause people to get in over their heads with their credit cards—not good. However, making those same mistakes on a grander scale can lead to the loss of your home . . . I think you get my point. Some states don't even allow home-equity loans—perhaps for good reason!

"When it comes to the deductibility of interest on investment loans there are a number of variables—you'd better consult an accountant." The way Roy stated this sounded more like a warning than a suggestion.

"Assuming we can structure our affairs in such a way that the interest on our consumer loans is tax-deductible, should we still pay off the loans?"

"Well, Cathy, it's really the same dilemma as whether or not paying off your mortgage is a good idea. I think the answer is yes, if it doesn't mean sacrificing your ten percent savings, insurance program, or retirement plans. When all factors are combined—a reasonable guaranteed after-tax rate of return, pride in ownership, a low PITA factor, an eventually freed-up cash flow, and reduced stress—you have a pretty attractive package. Besides which, even deductible interest, if you're paying enough of it, can kill your standard of living."

"Live within your means," my sister quietly reminded herself.

"There's another very interesting tax strategy I'd like to discuss: the batching of deductions. Let's assume that Dave and Sue, after itemizing, are just over the standard deduction—"

"We'll be way over, Roy, now that we have deductible mortgage interest," I corrected the wealthy barber.

181

"Are you cognizant of the meaning of the word 'assume,' Dave?"

No doubt Tom was thinking of throwing in his standard smart reply to Roy's question but the word "cognizant" slowed him down a little.

"A potentially clever maneuver would be to itemize your return every other year and to time your deductible expenses, as much as possible, to fall within those alternate years. By doing so, you would be limited to claiming only the standard deduction every second year, slightly less than you would have been entitled to claim in those years by itemizing, but in the 'itemizing years' you could save significant tax dollars."

"I'm not sure I follow," I admitted.

"Let's say 1992 was one of the years you were not going to itemize. In December of that year, hold off making charitable contributions, making your monthly mortgage payment, and paying local taxes, if allowed, until early 1993. Then in December of '93 make sure you make the 1993 donations, make your mortgage payment, and pay that year's local taxes. By doubling up on certain deductions every second year, you'll get the standard deduction half the time, temporarily sacrificing a little, but in the other years, when you itemize, you'll get a much bigger deduction. Assuming, of course, that this strategy is suited to your situation, the bottom line is that you'll save hundreds of dollars in taxes, and only have to go through the work of itemizing every second year!"

Roy was clearly deriving greater pleasure from dispensing this information than we were from receiving it.

"There are two related strategies that apply to miscellaneous deductions and medical expenses. Because both of these areas are only deductible to the extent that they exceed two percent and seven and a half percent of your adjusted gross income respectively, it may pay to bunch your expenses into certain years. By doing so—"

"We get it, Roy," Tom spoke for all of us. "Isn't all of this evidence of why it's so important to use the services of a professional?"

"Yes." Roy's one-word response indicated his frustration at having been cut off during a section he obviously took delight in.

"Seems like a lot of work," Cathy added. "Plus, I can't believe the IRS would be too excited about 'creative bunching.'"

"All right, all right . . . Let's move on," Roy conceded, a beaten but not broken man. "Another way to legitimately reduce your taxes is by going into business. In fact, many financial writers push this as the best way to save taxes. They point to the vast number of normally non-deductible expenses that may become deductible, or partially deductible, if you own your own business: your automobile, your computer, your travel, your phone, your entertainment, your children—yes, you heard me correctly —your magazine subscriptions, your VCR, et cetera. What is often not pointed out is that to become deductible these expenses must be incurred for business reasons. What is also seldom emphasized is that no business has ever become successful that was founded purely as a tax strategy.

"The argument that even an unsuccessful business, from a profit standpoint, can often be considered successful because it has transformed traditional personal expenses into legitimate tax deductions doesn't wash with me. There are a number of valid reasons to start up your own business, including the pursuit of profit, a desire for independence, a chance to meet people, and a sense of accomplishment. Potential tax savings, on the other hand, are not sufficient reason to start a business; they are instead a benefit of starting a business. It's very important that you always keep that distinction in mind. This is America—you should start a business if, and only if, you feel you have a product or service of value to produce.

"Now, let me get down off my soap box and add that starting your own business can, indeed, result in significant tax advantages, largely through the form of increased deductions. The key here is . . . " Roy paused to let us guess.

"Seek professional help!" I asserted confidently.

"Right on! For example, in your case, Dave, with Sue being a self-employed freelancer, in other words, owning her own business, there are many legitimate tax deductions she can claim that I'll bet you don't even know about."

"I realized that earlier, when James fired those questions at me about writing off some of my house, car, and computer expenses. Trust me, Roy, I'll check into it right away," I promised.

"OK, final tax point: Do some reading. I'm not trying to turn you into accountants or to bore you to death, but taking some time to at least skim a few of the books I'm about to recommend would be a good idea. Tax experts agree that the major mistake tax filers make is a basic one: They don't use all the available deductions. Yes, the professional advice you'll be getting will help, but so will the following books: Julian Block's *Year-Round Tax Strategies*, Sylvia Porter's *Tax-Saving Tips*, any tax guide by J. K. Lasser, and the IRS publication, *Your Federal Income Tax*. Of course, there are several other fine books as well, including—"

"Thanks for the advice," Tom interrupted. "Whew, can you believe how time flies? We'd best be going, Dave."

Normally I'd chastise Tom for being so rude, but in this case I was thankful—four tax guides is my limit. Actually, it's considerably over my limit.

"So, what's on the agenda for our last month, Roy?" Cathy wondered.

"There are four or five topics you still need a bit of information about. Then, of course, Clyde will present each of you with a hand-engraved, gold-trimmed diploma denoting your graduate status from the Miller School of Financial Planning. The diploma can either be wall-mounted or it can stand on a table—"

"Enterprising pupils probably scrape off the gold and sell it at the bank," interrupted the ever-enterprising Tom.

"I may have taught that lesson on thrift too well," Roy muttered, shaking his head.

Chapter 10

Graduation

"OH, YOU SHOULDN'T HAVE," CLYDE protested modestly. "I really didn't do all that much."

"Something tells me that that beautifully wrapped package isn't for you, Clyde," speculated James Murray. "It's for me."

"Nice try, guys." I chuckled. "This token of our appreciation is for Roy, in recognition of all he has done for us. Admittedly, you two, and even Jimmy here, have also been big helps to us in our quest for financial independence. For all you've done for us, we'd like to present you with our heartfelt thanks. We were going to buy each of you a gift, but as has been pointed out so often, 'A dollar saved is two dollars earned.'"

"Igor, vee've created a monster!" James Murray spoofed.

"You three really didn't have to buy me a gift," protested the blushing barber. "My reward is seeing you on the road to financial prosperity."

"That's exactly what I said, Roy, but Dave and Cathy wouldn't listen," Tom reported, straight-faced.

"Yeah, yeah . . . Dave, my boy, climb up into the chair and let's get started. There are four miscellaneous topics

I want to touch on and then, of course, there's my world-renowned wrap-up speech.

"Now, it really doesn't matter which of the four topics we start with. Let's kick off with emergency funds—"

"I was wondering when you would get around to that topic," Cathy jumped in. "Don't they always say that the average person should have a readily available emergency fund equivalent to four to six months' gross income?"

"Ah, the mysterious 'they' again," Roy sighed. "Many financial planners do recommend building and maintaining an emergency fund of that size, Cathy. However, I think, for a lot of us, that blanket advice is inappropriate. To me, it makes little sense to have upwards of ten thousand dollars sitting around earning fully taxable, low rates of return. In most cases, you would be much better off to use those funds to pay down your consumer debt or to fund your retirement plan. Really, with the exception of a job loss or, for the business owner and commissioned employee, an extended 'down period,' what emergency could possibly call for ten thousand dollars?"

"What if the wind blows the roof off your house one night?"

"You're covered by insurance."

"What if your car breaks down and needs repairs?"

"Ten thousand dollars' worth?"

"What if your furnace dies on the coldest night of the year?"

"Get it fixed," was Roy's uncomplicated advice. "It sure won't cost you ten grand. Look, I'm not opposed to emergency funds, but I do feel that two to three thousand dollars is a more prudent cushion than ten thousand. If you're afraid that an expensive emergency looms in your future, establish a ten-thousand-dollar line of credit at your bank. That way, if you really do end up needing the money, it will be there for you. In the meantime, you're free to invest your funds in more productive ways.

"Having said that, let me repeat that it is important to keep a few thousand at your fingertips. Minor emergencies not only can happen, they do happen! Especially if you're a homeowner! Also, if you have a couple of thousand in the bank and you see some item on sale that you really want, you can buy it. People with small bank balances are too often forced to pass up excellent bargains. And finally, having a couple of thousand dollars in the bank is good for your peace of mind. People sleep less soundly at night when they know that they have only one hundred and sixty-eight dollars in their account."

"What do you mean, 'only'?" Tom roared.

"Roy, you mentioned that a business owner might be wise to have a substantial emergency fund. Does that include me?" inquired Cathy.

"Obviously a business owner, or a commissioned salesperson whose income is unpredictable, varying widely over time, is smart to save for a rainy day. It's surprising the number of stockbrokers, for instance, who raise their standard of living during good times to match, or even to exceed, their temporarily high income level and don't set aside any funds to help carry them through the inevitable bad times. Cathy, whether or not your business should be considered cyclical in nature is your call.

"People who have little job security are also smart to maintain a substantial emergency fund. Again, of course, the decision rests with the individual involved. Frankly, someone like Tom has a much greater chance of being laid off than someone like Dave does. So, Tom should plan accordingly. It's really just common sense."

"Another thing worth keeping in mind here, Roy," James Murray took over, "is human nature. All too often it subverts the purpose of an emergency fund. The temptation to convert the emergency fund into a travel or boat fund is just too strong for most of us. The needs-versus-wants conflict again."

I could certainly see that happening!

188

"Another 'another' thing worth keeping in mind,"
James Murray continued eloquently, "is that although virtually all potential calamities should be covered by insurance protection, the insurance proceeds don't always
cover one hundred percent of the costs. For example, with
disability insurance there's often a waiting period before
benefits begin to be paid—the disabled party must cope
during that waiting period by dipping into his or her own
savings, in other words, his or her emergency fund. And
many health-insurance policies have co-insurance features
where the insurance company pays the lion's share of the
costs, but the insured party also pays a percentage. If a
major claim arose as a result of a lengthy illness, even a
small percentage of the total costs could be a lot of money.
Where's that money going to come from?

"Really, what I'm saying is that, in addition to the factors that Roy mentioned, the details of your various insurance policies may also play a role in determining the appropriate size of your emergency fund. That point being made,
I still agree that, for most of us, a few thousand is usually
sufficient, especially if a line of credit has been arranged."

"Important points, James, both of them," Roy acknowledged. "We'll talk more about disability and health
insurance in a few moments. Now on to miscellaneous
topic number two: saving for a child's college education."

"That shouldn't be hard," Tom interjected. "Don't do
anything and let the kids earn their way through school."

"How callous!"

"Not really, Cathy," I defended Tom. "There are all
kinds of parents, Mom and Dad among them, unfortunately, who believe that children should pay all, or at least
a major part of, the costs of a college education. I paid
my own way and, although I wasn't too thrilled with our
parents' stance at the time, I realize now that it was good
for me. I learned the value of hard work and self-discipline.
Today, I take pride in saying that I put myself through
school."

"What a martyr," Cathy snorted. "The only reason Mom and Dad didn't give you much help was that they were sure you were going to flunk out."

If I hadn't suspected that to be the case, I would have offered a scathing comeback.

"Regardless of the motives, there are, as Dave said, many parents who place on the child the bulk of the responsibility for paying for advanced schooling. In fact, I'm one of those parents. However, I will admit that, for a variety of reasons, it isn't always possible for the student to shoulder the entire burden. Colleges and universities are expensive, and getting more so at a greater-than-the-inflation-rate pace. Even a hard-working, independent student can't always raise the needed funds. This is especially true if, at an inopportune time, an economic downturn leads to a scarcity of good-paying summer jobs.

"So, although I feel that some of the saving responsibility should be the child's, I also feel parents should be willing and able to help out if needed."

"I see your point, Roy. I guess the key is not to have too many kids," I reasoned, only half-jokingly.

"Fortunately, there are a number of savings vehicles appropriate for creating a college fund," Roy resumed. "U.S. Savings Bonds offer several advantages: They are guaranteed by the federal government; the interest rate is adjusted every six months to keep you from being left behind by rising rates; and they can be purchased in denominations as small as twenty-five dollars.

"In addition to those benefits, some Savings Bonds may also receive preferential tax treatment. When the bonds are redeemed, if the adjusted gross income on the parents' joint return is less than sixty thousand dollars, the interest earned is tax-free. I should mention that that sixty-thousand-dollar threshold has been indexed to the inflation rate since 1990 . . . oh, and the threshold is forty thousand dollars for single or head-of-household filers. Over those limits, the tax break is gradually phased out.

"To get the tax break you must be age twenty-four or older when you buy the bonds, so obviously parents should register the bonds in their own names, not their child's.

"Even if you don't think you'll qualify for that tax break, U.S. Savings Bonds aren't a bad idea. They offer the three benefits I spoke of, and they're also exempt from state and local income taxes. Moreover, if you buy them in your child's name, an acceptable practice if you can't qualify for the tax break, and you redeem them after the child turns fourteen, the interest will be taxed at your child's rate. Unless he or she has become a rock star, that rate will be lower than your own.

"That last point is important enough to repeat— actually, rephrase. Once a child reaches age fourteen, all his or her income—including investment income—is taxed at his or her own rate."

"What about prepaid tuition plans, Roy?" I asked. "Some of my fellow teachers bought them for their children."

"Another interesting possibility," Roy began his reply. "The first important point to note is this: Although prepaid tuition plans definitely have some merit, they are not the 'almost painless' college-financing arrangement some people think they are.

"Generally speaking, the plans work like this: Years before a child's scheduled enrollment, parents pay a fixed sum determined by a number of variables, including the child's age, current tuition rates, and the state's estimates both of how much those rates will rise in the future and of the amount it expects to earn by investing the parents' funds. In return, the child is guaranteed four years at any public college in that state—regardless of how much costs rise."

"What if the state bases the prepayment amount on projections that costs will rise at only six percent a year and instead they rise at twice that pace?" I asked.

"That's their problem!" Tom answered unsympatheti-
cally.

"That's right, Tom, and because of that possibility you
can expect the states that offer these plans to use relatively conservative projections—they're not in this to lose
money. Their hope is to earn enough by investing the prepayment to offset future tuition increases," Roy explained.

"So, the major benefit of investing in a prepaid tuition plan is that, if tuition costs soar, we'll be protected,"
I summarized.

"Exactly," Roy confirmed, "exactly. There are some
drawbacks you should be aware of, though, the obvious
one being that prepaid tuition plans lock children into a
limited choice of schools. Michigan's plan is more liberal
than most, with only small penalties for attending out-
of-state colleges, but some other states' plans are very
rigid. Read the fine print!

"Also, be prepared to be hit with a big tax bill down
the road if you purchase one of these plans. In most states,
Michigan included, the parents have to pay tax on the difference between what they paid for the prepaid tuition
and the actual four-year costs when the child attends college. That difference can be substantial, and so can your
tax liability! You may be convinced that the IRS is unfair
in this regard, but that doesn't make saving enough money
to cover the tax liability any easier.

"Along with U.S. Savings Bonds and prepaid tuition
plans there are other financial products that are potentially useful when saving for your child's education.

"Some states are now offering tax-free municipal
bonds called baccalaureate bonds. Interest on them is exempt from federal, state, and local taxes and, like U.S. Savings Bonds, they can be purchased in small denominations.
For upper-income parents who aren't eligible for the U.S.
Savings Bond tax break, these could definitely be worth
a look, although I don't think they're available in Michigan . . . yet.

"There is even one bank that offers a CD with its interest rate linked to the inflation rate of college costs . . . not a bad idea!

"All things considered though, I still lean toward the following method: Purchase on a monthly basis a well-selected equity mutual fund for your child."

"Professional money management, the traditionally higher rates of return associated with long-term ownership, dollar cost averaging, forced savings . . . "

While Tom strained to prolong his display of knowledge, Roy resumed, "A child under the age of fourteen is currently allowed to earn five hundred and fifty dollars a year of investment income tax-free. The next five hundred and fifty dollars of investment income will be taxed at his or her own rate—in most cases, fifteen percent. Anything over that amount will be taxed at the parents' top rate. Those amounts, by the way, are indexed to inflation. After the age of fourteen—"

"All investment income is taxed at the child's rate," I remembered from earlier discussion.

"Now think about that for a moment." Roy paused.

"On top of all of the advantages Tom listed, equity funds are also ideal from a tax perspective. They'll normally pay a small annual dividend, depending on how much you've invested, of course, of much less than the five-hundred-and-fifty-dollar limit—therefore, no taxes payable! And if the fund is redeemed after the child turns fourteen, any capital gains are taxable in his or her hands, not the parents'.

"One word of caution here," Roy warned us. "Don't forget equity funds are long-term investments. If you choose them as a way to save for your child's education, it is best to begin the program when the child is young so there is time to ride out market fluctuations. Also, once your child is within a few years of college, I advise you to look for a good time to redeem the funds. As you know, markets don't go straight up, and if you wait to cash out until the day you actually need the money, Murphy's Law will guarantee that the markets will be down! That advice also holds for equities held inside your retirement plans."

"Makes sense," Tom concurred.

"All right, let's wrap up this section by looking at what may be the most popular, not to mention the most cost-efficient, way to save for your children's college education: Get family members, grandparents being one possible choice, to do it for you!"

"Makes even more sense," a thoughtful Tom concurred again.

"This advice is really all academic—pardon the pun. My kids are sure to be offered full scholarships," I proclaimed confidently.

"Nothing personal, Dave, but I'd do some saving just in case," Roy countered.

"I know you're anxious to move on, Roy, but I have a technical question," Cathy said apologetically. "How do we establish investments in our children's names?"

"In most cases you set up something called a custodial account. Parents—I'm assuming they've named themselves as custodians—select and manage the investments in the account. Be careful here, because once you've placed money in a custodial account, you can't reclaim it, and it must only be used for the benefit of the child."

"And even that's restricted, in that you can't use the money to help you to provide food, clothing, shelter, and other legally required items," James Murray elaborated.

"Why not just put the money directly into the child's name?"

"That's a possibility but it has two problems. One: If you go that route, the child could legally take control of the money at any age. Two: Certain investments, including mutual funds, are often difficult to purchase in a minor's name.

"Now on to—"

"Sorry, Roy," I interrupted, "but don't kids have direct access to custodial accounts, too?"

"Not until they reach the age of eighteen or twenty-one, depending on the state. By then, I'm sure your fine parenting skills will have had such a profound impact on your children that squandering the money won't even cross their minds. However, if you're worried, consult a lawyer or accountant about setting up a trust."

"One more thing, Roy," Tom jokingly started, before winking at the increasingly impatient barber.

"Miscellaneous topic number three: health and disability insurance," Roy pushed on.

"I'm confident that individuals as smart as you three recognize the importance of proper medical coverage. Unfortunately, millions don't. Nothing can wipe out your savings and throw your financial affairs into chaos more quickly than an uninsured major medical expense. Trust me, the numbers are downright scary. James?"

"That's right, Roy," James Murray agreed. "My brother's bill for a month-long stay in intensive care was over fifty thousand dollars. He was insured, thank goodness, but if he hadn't been . . . "

Scary stuff, indeed.

"I hope that, over the last few months, I've helped you three a lot," Roy began slowly. "If you want to pay me back, promise me this: Not only will you, by talking with your personnel department *and* an independent health-insurance agent, make sure that you currently have sufficient coverage, but also you'll review your coverage annually to make sure it's keeping up."

We all gave the thumbs-up sign.

"Although I'm sure you three recognize the importance of health insurance, I'm equally sure you don't recognize the importance of disability coverage," Roy continued.

"Disability insurance is the most neglected of all forms of insurance, yet, for many people, it's one of the most critical insurance needs. What are your chances of being disabled for a one-year period at some point in your life?"

"One in twenty?" Cathy guessed.

"I would say one in thirty," Tom speculated.

"One in four," Roy stated solemnly, taking the three of us aback.

Cathy broke our stunned silence. "That's amazing."

"It really is," Roy concurred. "A thirty-year-old has a one-in-four chance of becoming disabled for one year or more at some point in his or her life.

"At your age, your biggest asset, by far, is your earning power. You have to protect it. If a machine in your basement churned out forty thousand one-dollar bills a year, would you insure it against breakdown? Of course you would, especially if you knew there was a twenty-five percent chance that it would quit on you. Are you with me?"

We nodded our heads vigorously.

"When people die, they cease to be a financial asset to their dependents. That's why so many people need life insurance: to replace that asset—to replace that earning power. When people are disabled, they don't just cease to be an asset to their families—they become a liability. Excuse me for being blunt, but dead people don't need to be fed, clothed, or sheltered. Make sure that you have proper disability insurance coverage!"

"I'm covered through work," I announced. "You probably are too, Tom."

"Be careful about that assumption, Dave," Roy cautioned. "Many employer group plans offer insufficient coverage. In addition, they are often non-portable. If you left your place of work to go out on your own or to go to an employer who did not provide adequate group disability coverage, you would have to hope that you were in good enough health to qualify for an individual disability policy."

"How can I tell whether or not my group plan is adequate?"

"It isn't easy. Disability insurance policies are complex. However, there are some basic questions that you should seek answers to. If you receive a 'yes' to all of them, your policy would seem to be a good one. For example, is the loss of hearing, sight, speech, or of the use of two limbs considered to be total disability under your group policy? Is disability defined in broad terms? Is the policy non-cancelable? Is there a waiver-of-premium clause? If so, does it extend beyond the benefit period? Is the only policy exclusion an accident of war? Does the policy provide benefits during rehabilitation? Are the benefits indexed?"

"Slow down, Roy! Where do we find out about all this?" Tom took the words right out of my mouth.

"Talk to your personnel department. They should know the answers to most of those questions and, if they don't, they'll know where to find them. Also, show your group policy to an insurance agent who can help you compare its pros and cons with those of an individual policy."

"What if our group policies are inadequate?" Tom pressed on.

"If your group policy is inadequate, Tom, or if you are not even a member of one, you will have to buy an individual policy. Many life insurance agents are well versed in the area of disability insurance. Moreover, there are agents who specialize in designing disability insurance programs. Either source should be able to advise you on the plan and options best suited to your needs."

"Miscellaneous topic number four: staying informed," Roy moved on efficiently. "Yes, your financial plans are very straightforward in terms of both implementation and maintenance. But it certainly can't hurt to keep abreast of the major goings-on in the world of finance. Certain events could occur that might dictate a change in your planning philosophy. For example, the individual managing your mutual fund could die. You might then want to re-evaluate your choice.

"As I said months ago, there are several excellent sources of financial information available in the U.S., including *Forbes*, *Money*, *Fortune*, *Kiplinger's Personal Finance*, and, of course, the *Wall Street Journal*. These publications aren't just informative; they're also entertaining. The world of finance is dynamic, colorful, and fascinating!"

"Roy, can't you just do all the reading and keep us informed about anything pertaining to our financial futures?" Tom's idea sounded pretty good to me, but judging from the look of mock dismay on Roy's face, it didn't to him.

"All right, Clyde, drum roll, please. After seven long months, this is it. We've come to the end of the Miller course in financial planning. And, much to my delight, you have all passed with flying colors. However, before Clyde presents you with your diplomas, I'd like to make a closing remark . . . or two." Roy paused to step out from behind the barber chair.

"Over the last seven months I've taught you the basics of developing a sound financial plan. The strategies that I've outlined for you will serve well any American between the ages of twenty and forty-five. They will do so regardless of occupation; regardless of income level; regardless of previous financial knowledge; even regardless of mathematical, investment, and accounting skills.

"This comprehensive plan's strength lies in its simplicity. Anyone can understand and apply the principles that we've discussed. And, unlike most financial plans, ours goes beyond the mathematics of saving and investing to take into account human nature. Its success is not dependent on unrealistic expectations having to be met by the plannee, the way so many others are. I recognize that most people don't like to budget and that they don't enjoy constantly monitoring investments. I accept that most people enjoy blowing some money from time to time. I also understand that most people feel a great deal of stress when they are burdened with a high level of debt.

"The very simplicity of the plan troubles some people. 'How can anything so readily understood work so successfully?' It works because it is born of common sense. This plan allows us to move toward the attainment of all of our financial goals by taking advantage of unglamorous, but highly productive, concepts.

"Dave, when you first approached me, you said that you wanted to achieve the average American's goals of a nice home, a prosperous retirement, an education for your children, and at some point, you wanted to enjoy the finer things in life. You wanted to accomplish this without having to be a financial genius, and without a substantial reduction in your current standard of living. Do you feel that you have learned how?"

"Mission accomplished," I acknowledged appreciatively.

"The bottom line is simply this," Roy concluded. "Limited partnerships, straddle-option strategies, and future contracts on gold all make for great conversation at cocktail parties. Forced savings, dollar cost averaging, and compound interest simply make for great cocktail parties."

Roy's "bottom line," as he called it, was greeted with a standing ovation.

"Encore! Encore!" Tom shouted. "Teach us a family planning course now!"

"First, you'll have to find a wife, Tom. Now, please be seated," Roy protested. "Clyde, the certificates, please."

"You were serious about diplomas?" I asked, startled. "Wow, this is great! Hey, Tom, your first diploma!"

"Ha, ha!" Spending so much time at the barbershop had still not made Tom's comebacks razor-sharp.

Clyde proceeded to hand to each of us a beautifully framed, official-looking diploma from the Miller School of Financial Planning. He shook our hands and commended us for having taken the top three spots in our graduating class. Despite Clyde's kidding, the three of us were elated with our performance.

"As I'm sure you've noticed, we have a little something for you, too, Roy," I announced. Cathy presented Roy with a nicely wrapped package that obviously contained a framed picture.

Roy opened it deliberately, so as not to tear the gift wrapping.

"Going to reuse that paper at Christmas?" James Murray joked. "The virtue of thrift, and all that stuff."

When the picture was finally visible to him, Roy's eyes became misty. My talented sister had painted the front view of Roy's impressive house, capturing it in the warm glow of a sunset. The engraved gold plate adorning the frame read simply "The Rewards of Common Sense."

"This is wonderful . . . I'm deeply touched . . . I just love it. Marj will want it hung in the main living room, for sure. You shouldn't have," an emotional Roy insisted.

"It was the least we could do for our financial mentor," Cathy said sincerely. "We owe a great deal to you."

"In fact, we owe our good fortune," I added, smiling, "to *the wealthy barber!*"

The
Wealthy
Barber

Couldn't someone that you know benefit from reading *The Wealthy Barber?* It's the perfect gift for Americans between the ages of 20 and 45—understandable, enjoyable, and profitable!

Please rush me _____ copies of *The Wealthy Barber* at $17.95 each, including shipping. I have enclosed a check made payable to Financial Awareness Corporation in the amount of $_____ .

Full Name: _____

Address: _____

City: _____ State: _____

Zip Code: _____

Telephone #: _____

For an order of ten or more books we offer a discount. Please write to us for details, or call us at 1-800-665-3913. Visa and Mastercard orders accepted by phone.

FINANCIAL AWARENESS CORPORATION
c/o PRIMA PUBLISHING
P.O. Box 1260DC
Rocklin, CA
95677

The
Wealthy
Barber

Couldn't someone that you know benefit from reading *The Wealthy Barber?* It's the perfect gift for Americans between the ages of 20 and 45—understandable, enjoyable, and profitable!

Please rush me _____ copies of *The Wealthy Barber* at $18.95 each, including shipping. I have enclosed a check made payable to Financial Awareness Corporation in the amount of $ _____ .

Full Name: _____

Address: _____

City: _____ State: _____

Zip Code: _____

Telephone #: _____

For an order of ten or more books we offer a discount. Please write to us for details, or call us at 1-800-665-3913. Visa and Mastercard orders accepted by phone.

FINANCIAL AWARENESS CORPORATION
c/o PRIMA PUBLISHING
P.O. Box 1260BK
Rocklin, CA
95677